MARGARET CHO

ASIAN AMERICANS
OF ACHIEVEMENT

ASIAN AMERICANS
OF ACHIEVEMENT

MARGARET CHO

CAROLINE TIGER

CHELSEA HOUSE
PUBLISHERS
An imprint of Infobase Publishing

Margaret Cho

Copyright ©2007 by Infobase Publishing

Chelsea House
An imprint of Infobase Publishing
132 West 31st Street
New York, NY 10001

Library of Congress Cataloging-in-Publication Data
Tiger, Caroline.
   Margaret Cho / Caroline Tiger.
       p. cm. — (Asian Americans of achievement)
   Includes bibliographical references and index.
   ISBN 0-7910-9275-5 (hardcover)
   ISBN-13 978-0-7910-9275-0
1. Cho, Margaret.   2. Comedians—United States—Biography.
3. Asian American comedians—Biography.   I. Title.   II. Series.
   PN2287.C537T54 2007
   792.702'8092—dc22
   [B]

                           2006028385

Text design by Erika K. Arroyo
Cover design by Ben Peterson

Printed in the United States of America
Bang NMSG 10 9 8 7 6 5 4 3 2 1

This book is printed on acid-free paper.

All links and Web addresses were checked and verified to be correct at the time of publication. Because of the dynamic nature of the Web, some addresses and links may have changed since publication and may no longer be valid.

CONTENTS

Reason for Being

When Margaret Cho was 15 years old, she was a devoted member of the "Cutting Club." Although her parents would see her leave every morning for the bus, with her backpack swung into place, she never actually arrived at school. Instead, she hung out with the other "bad kids," drinking alcohol and smoking pot and hanging out at their houses while their parents were at work. In fact, there were entire semesters when she didn't go to class—and she never tried to make up the work she missed. She cared very little about school. She had a 0.6 GPA (the consequence of all F's and one Incomplete). Not surprisingly, Lowell High expelled her. Lowell was a magnet school—it was filled with some of the smartest kids in San Francisco's public school system. It makes sense that a school for above-average students would not tolerate behavior like Margaret's.

Her mother, Young Hie Cho, and father, Suen Hoon Cho, were surprised and distraught. They placed a great deal of importance on education. They were always telling Margaret how much they had sacrificed of their own lives, moving from Korea to America and working hard, so she and her brother could go to good schools. It looked to them like she was throwing away all of their hard work. In her autobiography, *I'm the One That I Want*, Cho wrote that being expelled was "totally unacceptable for a nice Korean girl like myself." Of course, she had never fit the stereotype of a "nice Korean girl," but her parents still hoped she might overnight turn into that stereotype: a quiet, studious, obedient girl who plays concert-level violin or piano and never earns a grade below an A in school. They might not have cared that she was noisy and disobedient if she had brought home a report card full of A's. Good grades seemed to matter more to them than anything else. When one of Margaret's classmates went to prison for stabbing someone at a 7-11 convenience store, her father said to her, "At least he had good grades."

Even if she didn't let it show, Margaret, too, was upset over being expelled. She felt like a failure. Many years later, though, looking back, she knew that being forced out of Lowell was a blessing in disguise. For one thing, she had never fit in there. The boys ignored her, and the girls were mean to her. Plus, she was getting bored with the Cutting Club's same old activities.

In addition, as Cho points out in her typically outrageous and hilarious way, it was actually to her advantage to disappoint her parents so completely, so early on. "It [gave me] a kind of freedom that really propelled me into the life I have now," she wrote in her autobiography. "I didn't have to impress anyone. I didn't have to go to a good school. I had nothing left to do but pursue my dreams. In a sense I had nowhere else to go." If Margaret hadn't hit rock bottom at age 15, she may never have discovered her passion for comedy, which would ultimately propel her to stardom and would end up saving her from herself many times over.

After years of practice, Margaret Cho now feels most comfortable on stage, making people laugh.

After Margaret was expelled, she had the summer to decide what to do. She found out that nearby San Francisco State University was offering a summer-stock theater program for high-school students. By this point in her life, performing was already a secret desire. At night, she had very vivid dreams about being on stage—and being really good at it. She knew she would be a successful performer. She could just feel it. She kept it a secret, though, because she also knew her parents would not approve. She knew they would say, "Koreans don't do that!" She had no evidence to throw back at them to show that she could do it, because her talents at that point were untested. There was nothing else for her to do that summer, though, so her parents said it was OK to join the theater program.

For the first time in her academic career, Margaret was not a total outcast. The other teens at the summer-stock program were just as "different" as Margaret was. It didn't take long for her to make friends—with Claudia, a girl with a shaved head who was into punk rock music; Lauren, a beautiful and dramatic redhead; and Alexi, a blond who called herself a Communist. Through this program and these relationships, Margaret gained some self-confidence and found the inner courage to try out for the School of the Arts (SOTA) high school. She had assumed she would continue high school at Lincoln, the public school nearest her house. It was Alexi's idea that she audition for SOTA, a high school for kids who want to pursue careers in the visual and performing arts.

Margaret prepared a monologue from *Runaways*, a play cowritten in 1975 by playwright Elizabeth Swado and a group of actual runaways or "problem" teenagers. The original play, a collection of songs and monologues, was staged in New York and starred some of the former runaways who cowrote the script. Margaret chose a monologue, memorized it, and auditioned. She was accepted into SOTA's Class of 1987.

SOTA was much different from Lowell High. Margaret already had friends at SOTA, and she soon made more. "I was with the theater crowd," she recalled in a 2001 magazine interview with the *Tablet*. "I was chubby and loud and carried a lunchbox. And wore striped tights. I was very popular in theater but not in school proper. I totally wore a lot of white girl makeup with superarched eyebrows and red lipstick. Like total pre-goth, super early '80s goth."

Margaret spent every day with kids who shared her passion for performing and her dream to become an actor. In the halls, there were dancers in tights standing with their feet turned out, like they were still in ballet class. She felt like her life had turned into the movie *Fame*, which was about a group of kids who go to the Performing Arts High School in New York City. She loved that her life resembled a cool movie.

When Margaret started at SOTA, she wanted to be an actor, but somewhere along the way, she changed her mind and decided to become a comedian. Watching Richard Pryor's live concert film *Live on the Sunset Strip* really convinced her. When she saw the film, she thought, "Wow, that's it." She realized comedy was her destiny. Margaret was immediately inspired by Pryor, an African-American stand-up comedian and actor known for his raw, straightforward—and often expletive-laced—observations about racism in America. He was one of the first stand-up comedians who injected social commentary into his act, something that would later become a hallmark of Cho's standup.

At SOTA she joined an improv comedy group called Batwing Lubricant. Improv groups don't work from a script; the actors improvise the dialogue as they go along. It is very difficult to perform, especially "spot improv," in which the audience yells out suggestions for the subject of the actors' next skit. To Margaret, it may have felt difficult, but it also felt deliciously right, especially when they took their act out for a spin.

The stand-up comedy scene was booming in San Francisco in the 1980s and 1990s. There were a lot of clubs like the Other Café and the Holy City Zoo, where comics honed their skills onstage. Los Angeles, the center of the TV and entertainment industry, was a short drive, so the comics in San Francisco were always hoping a scout would show up and see them on a night when they *killed* (a stand-up comedy term for "doing really well"). For them, the ultimate sign of success would be to land their own TV show, as Roseanne Barr and Jerry Seinfeld had done.

When Margaret was 16, she and Batwing Lubricant performed as part of a Showcase Night at the Other Café. It was daunting to know that she was going to do her act on a stage that was frequented by very successful stand-up comics like Robin Williams, Paula Poundstone, Bobcat Goldthwaite, Dana Carvey, and Dennis Miller. Batwing Lubricant killed, and they

Margaret Cho has always admired the frank and funny comedy of legend
Richard Pryor, seen here performing in 1977.

were invited back for another night. It was a life-changing experience. "I saw, in that dark and smoky club, the rest of my life," Cho wrote in her memoir. "I thought if I could just be allowed to go onstage and make people laugh every night, that I wouldn't care if I made money or became famous. Just the ability to do it would be payment enough." Margaret Cho's dreams were coming true.

Outsider in a City of Outsiders

Margaret Cho was born on December 5, 1968, in San Francisco. Just three days after her birth, her father was deported to Korea. Her mother was unable to provide for a baby on her own, so she sent the four-month-old to Seoul to live with her grandparents. Later, her mother showed her a photo of an elderly Korean woman wearing a white, Korean *hanbok*. "She was your auntie," her mother told her. "She take care of you when you baby." (Cho always quotes her mother faithfully, heavy Korean accent and all.) Margaret's grandfather on her father's side converted to Christianity and became a Methodist minister. He opened his home to refugee children and ran an orphanage in Seoul during the Korean War (1950–1953). Margaret got her first taste of show business when she saw her grandfather in his minister's robes and noted how his parishioners listened to him preach with peaceful smiles on their faces.

Margaret's mother, Young Hie Cho, was born into a wealthy family in Korea, and her parents arranged for her to marry a specific young man, as was the custom. Their offer did not interest her, however. Maybe it was the consequence of absorbing Western culture when she lived in Paris in the early 1960s. Maybe it was because she was in love. It could have been a combination of both. Whatever was at the root, Young Hie ignored the rigid traditions of Korea's patriarchal culture. She resisted the arranged marriage and instead wed Margaret's father, converting from Buddhism to Christianity. Even so, "She never ever lost her ever-loving kindness, compassionate, reincarnatin' ways," wrote Cho. "This blend of spirituality [Christianity with Buddhism] resulted in a practical, nonjudgmental outlook. It had all the benefits of Christianity, but with a third less fat, and even less sentimentality." Cho described her family's religious beliefs on her personal Weblog as "a fairly hard scrabble Christianity with an austere flavor of Zen Buddhism. Lots of rules, no sentimentality."

Margaret Cho's family has a tradition of strong women. In her book, *I Have Chosen to Stay and Fight*, she wrote an essay about a great-great grandmother with whom she shares a trait—her "dinky pinkies," or pinky fingers so small they appear as if there are joints missing. This woman, she wrote, was a "notorious and riotous great wildebeest of a woman" with hair that remained midnight-black until she died at age 122. Among other scandalous traits, this ancestress wore pants (a shocking thing in those days), and her laugh was loud enough to be heard from miles away. She was good-natured but fierce when it came to protecting her family. "I have this biological legacy to live up to her legend, to carry on her work, of compassion, protection, defiance and laughter," wrote Cho, "To grow my hair and not be afraid of my village's judgment and ridicule, of my 'ugliness,' hugeness, my ability to conform, my delicate manner, my loud and resounding laugh. . . . That my hands are small makes no difference."

Margaret's mother and father left Korea in 1964 and settled in California, where her father earned a business degree and found work as an auditor. Margaret's father, Suen Hoon Cho, also wrote joke books in Korean. "Books like *1001 Jokes for Public Speakers*—real corny stuff," Cho said. "I guess we're in the same line of work. But we don't understand each other that way. I don't know why the things he says are funny and the same for him."

By the time Margaret returned to America, she was three years old, and she had become used to caretakers who weren't her parents. Back in San Francisco, she and her parents and aunt and uncle all lived together for a while in one apartment. Her father spent a lot of time in Korea, though, so her strongest memories are of her mom and aunt, and of watching TV. Her parents worked a lot, so TV was her babysitter. What came first—her strong instinct to become a performer or watching performers on TV? She's not sure, but both happened early. Her earliest memories include seeing Richard Nixon, U.S. president from 1969 to 1974, on television.

Even as a little kid, Margaret had a rebellious streak—she once stole a bottle of Binaca Blast from the convenience store owned by her aunt and uncle. At her Catholic nursery school, she was always getting into trouble for finger-painting her neighbor or for crawling around when she was supposed to be napping. Another time, she "ruined" the school Christmas pageant by waving to her mother and aunt in the audience, after the class had been told many times not to wave to anyone. Even at an early age, she was outgoing and looking for attention—she and her mom took the bus everywhere, and she was always saying "hi" to strangers. "I learned early on," she wrote, "that if you smiled at people, it increased your chances of [getting] candy."

All in all, Cho does not consider her childhood a happy one. Her father was away much of the time, and when he *was* around, her parents bickered frequently. She describes her parents' marriage as tense and unhappy. (It improved much later, however, after Margaret had grown up and moved out of the house.) In addition, Margaret didn't make friends easily. She remembers being teased mercilessly for peeing in her pants during a rehearsal for the third-grade Christmas concert.

Margaret was also teased because of her name. She was born Moran Cho—in Korean, Moran means "peony flower," which is a hardy, beautiful flower that blooms year-round in Korea, even surviving through the harshest winters. The other kids in school didn't know about her name's meaning, and, if they had, they probably would not have cared. They just knew that "Moran" was one letter away from "moron." When she was 12, the kids at her church started calling her "Moron." "Moron! Moron!" they'd yell. When she arrived, they would say, "Oh, no. Moron's here."

During one miserable church retreat, when the whole group went camping, the kids threw pinecones at Margaret. Then they filled her sleeping bag with leaves and twigs and acorns. Worst of all, they ignored her and didn't want to talk to her or even sit near her. After she returned home from that camping trip, she refused to ever go to that church again. Margaret was happiest in the summertime when she left San Francisco to visit her cousins at their house in Glendale. They would sit by the pool reading magazines like *Teen Beat* and *Seventeen*.

Cho could not help but notice, however, that none of the girls in these magazines or on her beloved TV shows looked anything like her. She wrote:

> One of my earliest memories . . . is the day I realized I was not white and therefore not like the people I saw on TV. I was looking in the mirror and saw for the first time that the reflection was me. Who was this odd-looking creature with the black hair and small, black eyes? Why wasn't I like Cindy Brady? . . . Why were all the people on TV who looked like me foreign or ancient or fortune-tellers or servants or soldiers?

Cho saw Asian Americans all over the place in her day-to-day life, in Japantown, at school—everywhere—except on

Between the Generations
KOREAN IMMIGRATION IN U.S. HISTORY

Korean immigrants came to America in three major waves during the twentieth century. On January 13, 1903, 120 Korean men, women, and children arrived in Honolulu Harbor via the S.S. *Gaelic*. They came to work as low-wage laborers on the sugar plantations of Hawaii. About 7,000 more Korean immigrants (mostly men) followed in the next few years. Japanese domination of Korea was causing great unrest and political turmoil at home, so America was a welcome alternative. About 1,000 women immigrated from Japan and Korea to marry the male laborers who had moved to America. Before they arrived by ship, the future husbands and wives had only seen each other's photographs.

This flow of people from the East ended in 1924, when growing anti-Asian sentiment in America prompted the government to pass an act that put an end to immigration from Asia. The Japanese continued to rule over Korea until the United States and its Allies defeated Japan in World War II in 1945. At this time, Korea was divided into two independent countries, North Korea and South Korea. The war-torn countries were taken under wing, respectively, by the Soviet Union and the United States. The Soviet Union installed a Communist government in the North, and the United States helped instate a democratic government in the South. A civil war between the two halves erupted into the multinational Korean War, with both sides fighting for total control from 1950 to 1953. In 1953, an armistice was reached, and the North and South were again established as separate countries.

Emigration from Korea to America began again after World War II. The U.S. government passed the War Brides Act of 1946, which allowed U.S. servicemen stationed overseas to bring their foreign wives home. In 1952, the McCarran-Walter Act reopened America's borders to small numbers of Asian immigrants, with preference given to skilled professionals and students. Because of these two laws, immigrants from Korea between 1951 and 1964 mostly included war brides from the Korean War, war orphans adopted by Americans, and professional workers and students.

President Lyndon Johnson signed the Immigrant Act of 1965 on October 3 of that year. The act was a huge turning point. For the first time, immigrants from all over the world were permitted to enter the country in large numbers and study to become U.S. citizens. Koreans took advantage of the opportunity: From 1965 on, one in every three Asian immigrants was Korean. By 1975, the number of Korean immigrants who had settled in America increased to more than 30,000. Because they didn't learn English before they arrived, though, many immigrants were unable to secure jobs in the occupations for which they were trained (e.g., lawyers, doctors, engineers, teachers). Many, like Margaret's parents, opened and ran their own small businesses, which were often retail outlets such as greengrocers and bookshops.

During the 1980s, the Korean-American population doubled and grew to make up 12 percent of the Asian-American population. Since 1987, however, fewer Koreans have emigrated because of improvements in South Korea's economy and also because, after race riots erupted between African Americans and Korean Americans in Los Angeles in 1992, many feel that living in the United States is unsafe.

television or in the magazines that pictured the people she admired. She started to think that maybe there was something wrong with her. Much later in her life, she'd tell an interviewer, "I've always been a reject. I've always been too loud and unpleasant to look at and unpleasant to listen to and just altogether wrong."

When Margaret was five years old, her brother, Hahn Earl, was born, and the family moved out of the aunt and uncle's apartment and into their own house in the Sunset District. Margaret's parents began to run a snack bar in a bowling alley in San Francisco's Japantown. Margaret started elementary school at the Dudley Stone School, now called the William R. Deavila School. She wrote, "[San Francisco] was different than any other place on Earth. I grew up and went to grammar school on Haight Street during the '70s. There were old hippies, ex-druggies, burnouts from the '60s, drag queens, and Chinese people. To say it was a melting pot—that's the least of it. It was a really confusing, enlightening, wonderful time."

In the late 1960s, the Haight was home to a lot of famous rock bands, including Janis Joplin, the Grateful Dead, and Graham Nash. It was a popular meeting place for hippies (young people who rebelled against the establishment by growing their hair long, wearing brightly colored clothes, taking illegal drugs, and refusing in general to conform to the government's and their parents' standards). In 1967, the Haight became the gathering place for thousands of "flower children" (another name for hippies), when that summer was proclaimed the Summer of Love. Just a year before Margaret was born in San Francisco, hippies descended on the city from all over the country. They held music festivals and poetry readings and listened to speeches denouncing America's involvement in the Vietnam War. Many of the people who came that summer stayed in San Francisco and continued to hang around the Haight.

San Francisco is very much a city of distinct neighborhoods. In addition to the hippies in the Haight, various ethnic

Cho's parents ran a snack bar in a bowling alley in San Francisco's Japantown. The distinct and colorful neighborhoods of Cho's youth would provide her with a lot of comedy material.

groups congregated (and continue to congregate) in different areas of the city. Japantown, where Margaret's parents worked, was settled by the descendants of thousands of Japanese people, who began to immigrate to California in the 1860s. San Francisco also has a Chinatown and a Koreatown. In addition, in the 1960s and 1970s, a growing number of gay men began to buy houses in a neighborhood called the Castro, so that area became known as the city's gay neighborhood.

When she was 10, Margaret's parents sold the bowling-alley snack bar and bought a bookstore, Paperback Traffic, on Polk Street. In the 1970s, Cho later wrote, Polk Street was "the Promised Land for homosexual men from all over the world." At first, Margaret didn't understand what homosexuality was—she knew that men fell in love with women and vice versa, but she didn't know there were other possibilities. Her mother explained it to her as best as she could, and soon she began to figure out that homosexuals fall in love with people of the same gender—men with men and women with women. When she realized that the men hanging around her parents' store weren't interested in her in a romantic or sexual way, she suddenly felt very safe. Margaret's body had started to develop, and she didn't like the way men were staring at her new curves. The idea that she could be around a group of men who did not want to gawk at her body made her feel protected and calm.

Dante and Forbes were her first gay pals. They worked at Paperback Traffic. Dante was thin, with a shaved head, dangly earrings, a soft voice, and a shy smile. Forbes was tall and thin, and he spoke with a British accent. Tattoos covered most of his body. They recommended good books for her to read, and they introduced her to drag queens—men who dress up like women—and to makeup. She became inseparable with a gay classmate, Berry, who was in her high-school theater group. She felt drawn to him. "I was a loud, fat girl and saw as my natural companion the fey, lithe boy," she wrote. "We were both scared. Thank God we met." Because she and they found themselves outside the mainstream, they shared a feeling of "otherness."

In the 1970s, the gay-rights movement intensified in response to growing discrimination against homosexuals. The

Cho remembers vividly when San Francisco City Supervisor Harvey Milk, a gay political leader and activist, was killed, along with the city's mayor, George Moscone.

tension dated from the 1950s, when President Eisenhower passed a law that barred gay Americans from working for the federal government. State and local governments, and corporations, followed suit. These actions sent a message to the rest of the country. Gay people were made to feel ashamed. Those who didn't attempt to keep their sexual identities a secret were harassed. Police raided gay bars across the country. In response, many gay Americans began to organize and fight back. The Castro became the locale for some tense clashes between gay-rights activists and the police.

It hurt Margaret to see her gay friends suffer discrimination just because they were a little different. When she was eight, Harvey Milk, the first openly gay man to be elected to political office in the United States, was shot and killed in San Francisco. "I think it changed my view of the way the world is," she told an interviewer later. "It showed me how much hatred is in the world." In her teens, she watched many of her friends from Polk Street, including her two best friends during high school, waste away from the AIDS virus. She said later that it was like being at the center of a holocaust.

3

On the Road

What types of people become comics or comedians? It is a commonly held belief that comedians spring forth from unhappy childhoods. "Comedy is tragedy plus time": This is one of those well-worn quotes that has been uttered so many times by so many people that no one knows anymore who said it first. The notion of comedians suffering through unhappy childhoods certainly applies to one of Margaret Cho's heroes, Richard Pryor, who was raised in his grandmother's brothel. Jim Carrey, too, had it pretty rough as a kid. His family struggled to make ends meet, and his mother suffered from depression, so he was constantly trying—and failing—to cheer her up.

Like most stereotypes, however, the idea that comedians' childhoods are horrendous might be more of an exaggeration than a rule. It seems more common that comedians face typical (rather than tragic) obstacles as kids. Sarah Silverman had a perfectly fine childhood, except for a bed-wetting problem. Robin Williams was overweight and shy, and he was picked on by bullies—things that happen to many kids. Adam Sandler was the only one of his siblings who didn't do well in school, but he was always good at making people laugh.

So where does Margaret Cho fit in? She is probably a little closer to tragic than to typical. She had a tough time dealing with teasing by other children at school and at church, and with her parents' tense, unstable marriage. She didn't measure up to society's definition of "pretty": She didn't look anything like the blonde, perky girls on TV and in magazines, and she wasn't dainty or skinny like those girls. She didn't measure up to her parents' standards, either: They wanted her to get all A's in school. Finally, her own body betrayed her: She developed earlier than other girls her age, which prompted unwelcome gawking and touching by older men far before she was ready for that kind of attention.

These experiences all contributed to Cho's illegal drug use in high school—first, she abused alcohol and marijuana, and she would do so again in her 20s. Comedy kept her from losing herself completely to alcohol and drugs, however. While she was onstage, she couldn't be high; she had to be completely aware and awake.

After high school, Cho was rejected by colleges, but that did not matter much to her. She was only interested in comedy. When she was 16, a friend dared her to take the stage at open-mike night at the Rose & Thistle, a club upstairs from her parent's bookstore. Once she did, she was hooked. The comedy clubs became her new classroom. She still worked with her parents during the day at Paperback Traffic, but at night she performed at the Rose & Thistle. She also went to shows at the Punchline, the Other Café, and other clubs to watch and learn from established comics. Her first attempts were not great. Friends who came to see her said things like, "It's really brave of you to get up there in front of all those people" instead of "you killed." Every time she went onstage, though, she learned and she improved.

Margaret started performing in 1984, but her parents didn't see her onstage until 2000. It was almost like they did not want

COMEDY: MUCH MORE THAN
A SUM OF ITS JOKES

For Margaret Cho, comedy is much more than a means for getting a laugh or two. Comedy is healing for her to write and perform, and she hopes it is also healing for audiences to hear. "I don't think what I'm doing for some people is just entertainment," she said. "I think it's a way of feeling like we belong in the world and a way to feel validated, so I don't take their support of me lightly."

Once Cho has had time to digest an experience, she is likely to use it in her act. "A lot of my material comes out of my own pain. It's like they say, 'Comedy is tragedy plus distance.'" While she's writing her material, the only aspects of her life that are off limits are the things that are happening to her at the moment. "In general, I don't feel like talking about something until I'm done with it," she said. "If it's happening, it's too raw." When she performs for an audience, she wants to hear that people are laughing from the gut. "We see someone who's a success at personal healing, at authentic healing and gives the possibility for universal healing," said artist Noreana Abookire about Cho, "She does not preach, she does not demean anyone, she simply speaks the truth."

Comedy is Cho's way of sharing her experience growing up as a minority person in America. She is an "other" in so many ways—as an Asian-American woman, as a person of size, as a bisexual person—and she's interacting with society in a specific cultural moment. Sharing her experience with audiences and recording them for future audiences is also a way of handing down an oral history to the next generation. Cho said, "There are few narratives of Asian Americans in the media, so we have to create [them] ourselves; it's a way of preserving what happened and documenting it."

to see her onstage, because that would make it more real—and they did not want it to be real. They did not consider comedy an appropriate career, so they tried to discourage her. They told her that Korean people could never be entertainers, that it just was

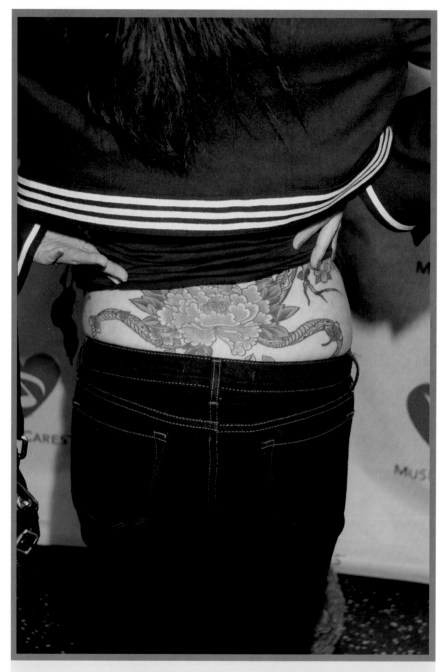

Cho has always been unconventional. Here she shows off her lower back tattoo as she arrives at the second annual MusiCares MAP Fund Benefit Concert.

not possible. "They did not see any evidence of anyone like me succeeding, and they didn't want the world to disappoint me," Cho said in a newspaper interview in 2001. "Asians put a high emphasis on education and conservative careers because of fear; then we, their children, wind up not pursuing our dreams because of our parents' racial vision." If Cho had pursued her parents' dreams, she surely would have failed. She pursued her own, though, and this made all the difference, although her path was never an easy one.

The established comedians at the San Francisco clubs she frequented were not a welcoming group. The first time she performed at the Punchline, she was afraid to go into the green room (the room backstage where the performers hang out before and after their sets). She remembers that the green room was filled with grown men, who all acted like they'd known each other for years and who were having a great time smoking, talking, and laughing about their performances and about the crowd. Cho was afraid to enter the room, so she hovered outside the door. No one noticed her, and if they did, they did nothing to make her feel welcome. Being made to feel like an outsider made her more determined to belong in the entertainers' world.

At first, stand-up comedy was really scary for Cho. The whole day before she was to go on, she worried about what she was going to say, what the crowd would be like. Would there even be a crowd? She fantasized about calling the club to say she was sick or that her dog had eaten her jokes. The anxiety would build and build until her spine was tingly, her hands were shaky, and she just felt like running away. Then, the emcee would call her name, and she would surprise herself by walking out in front of the crowd and getting out her first joke.

"Most of the time, it would go fine," she wrote, "and people would laugh and I'd stand a little taller and feel a little more confident. Sometimes, I wasn't very good. Time would drag and I'd leave the stage defeated, but it never felt as bad as I thought it

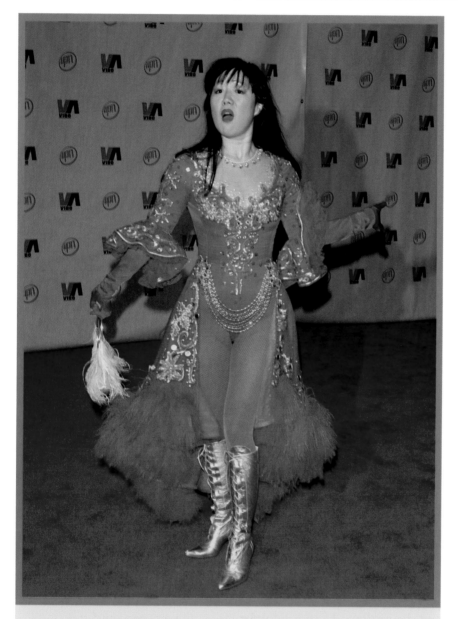

Cho took a while to find her style, which she calls "outrageous diva," certainly in evidence here as she arrives at the 2003 Vibe Awards.

would." If it went badly, she'd try to get onstage again as soon as possible, to erase the performance and replace it in her memory with a better one. Eventually, she met other people who were hovering in the hallway outside the green room, and one day the green room was empty, so they all went inside and sat down. When Cho saw unfamiliar people standing timidly by the door, she was the first to invite them in.

To save money, at first, Cho continued to live at her parents' house. She worked at their bookstore and at an FAO Schwarz toy store and did other odd jobs to support her burgeoning comedy career. After an exhausting day going from one job to the next, she came home, changed out of the Raggedy Ann outfit she put on to work at FAO Schwarz, and went out to the clubs. After a little while, Cho began going on the stand-up circuit, playing one-night engagements in the late 1980s at clubs all over California. She wasn't making a lot of money, but it seemed like a lot at the time. She considered herself especially lucky when she played comedy night at Sweetriver Saloon, where she earned $50 plus a $12 food ticket.

Cho hadn't yet discovered her style. She was in the early stages of her act, still evolving, still trying on different personas. "At that time, I was learning to be an outrageous diva," Cho wrote. This meant dressing the part. She glammed it up onstage, wearing pink wigs, rhinestone bowties, and long black gloves decorated with red bows. The women of Second City, a comedy troupe in Toronto, were some of her strongest role models. She watched their TV show, Second City Television (*SCTV*). "I think I would have died if I didn't have *SCTV*," Cho told an interviewer. "It just really did it for me, even more so than *Saturday Night Live*, because there were so many women that were important—Andrea Martin, Catherine O'Hara, Robin Duke."

Well-known female comics in the late 1980s tended to wear jackets with big shoulder pads and put on a kind of bawdy, wisecracking persona, so Cho did, too. For several years, she drove to small clubs in the American suburbs, testing out her act, hoping for the occasional TV spot on a late-night show, hoping to be discovered and—the dream of all dreams—to be offered her own sitcom.

In 1991, she was named Champion of the West Coast Division in the U.S. College Comedy Competition, a comedy contest where first prize was opening for Jerry Seinfeld in Daytona

CHO'S EARLY INFLUENCES

Cho told an interviewer in 2002, "It's weird to be categorized as an Asian comic, because I'm kind of like the only one in the file. . . . There's not like a big, bulging manila folder filled with, like, Hongs and Tanakas, you know." With no Asian-American role models to look up to, Cho instead looked up to stand-up comedians like Richard Pryor, a great comic who blazed a trail for future comics to be honest, confessional, and socially conscious.

Cho first became hooked on comedy in part because she watched Richard Pryor's concert film, *Live on the Sunset Strip*. Pryor was one comedian with a decidedly tragic childhood. His mother was a prostitute, and he was raised in the brothel his grandmother ran in Peoria, Illinois. Pryor grew up black and poor in the 1940s and 1950s, when movie theaters still forced blacks to sit in a separate area from whites. He was expelled from school at age 14 and went on to work a series of minimum-wage jobs before breaking into New York's comedy scene in the 1960s. His comedy riffed on these experiences of being part of the black underclass in America and dealing with life on the streets. He also dealt with racism. He delved deep into his own tragedies for his socially astute, confessional stand-up material. In his routines, he addressed his drug addiction, numerous marriages, two heart attacks, and diagnosis with multiple sclerosis. In a letter to Pryor on her blog, Cho wrote, "I owe a great debt to you, because I carry on what you did so beautifully, and I try to think 'What would Richard Pryor do?'

Beach, Florida. Seinfeld encouraged Cho to continue on the path she was on. If she did, he said, she was guaranteed to be a star. This exposure garnered some TV spots, on *Evening at the Improv* and on an offshoot of *Star Search* called *Star Search International*, which featured foreign performers. They asked Cho to represent Korea, which she thought was ridiculous, since she had been born in America and felt in all respects more

Many comics follow in your footsteps, but you got the huge shoes to fill."

SCTV, or Second City Television, also influenced Cho. *SCTV* ran for seven seasons and won two Emmys. The show originated as a regular skit performed by the Toronto-based faction of the Chicago-based comedy troupe Second City. The skit, which took place in a fictional TV station, became a TV show in 1977. The cast included Eugene Levy, Catherine O'Hara, Andrea Martin, Robin Duke, and Rick Moranis. Cho especially found it inspiring to see so many funny women gathered on her favorite place—the TV screen.

Finally, Cho was inspired by the comedian Steve Martin. Martin was born in Waco, Texas, to a real-estate salesman dad and a housewife mom. His first job in entertainment was playing the banjo, making balloon animals, and doing tricks at the Magic Shop in Disneyland, as a teenager. He went to college at California State and majored in philosophy but dropped out. In 1967, he got a job as a writer for the *Smothers Brothers Comedy Hour* and together with the other writers, won an Emmy Award in 1969. He performed his own material as an opening act for rock bands. He became famous in the 1970s when the stand-up he performed on the *Tonight Show* with Johnny Carson landed him a regular spot on *Saturday Night Live*. In his stand-up and his writing—he wrote the screenplays for *Roxanne*, *The Jerk,* and *L.A. Story*—his style is a mix of self-mockery, social commentary, and totally wacky physical humor.

American than Korean. As Cho recalled in her memoir, the show's coordinator asked her to act more authentic. She asked Cho, "Could you be more oh, I don't know, *Chinese*?" Of course, Cho is not Chinese. She is Korean-American. When Cho appeared onscreen, a little Korean flag flew next to her name. "Having to factor in the color of my skin whenever I tried to do anything really frustrated me," she wrote later. "It is not that I was ashamed of my background, but that was all anybody could see at first."

Before she was to appear on an episode of the *Montel Williams Show*, she was snubbed by the make-up artist. He powdered her nose for a quick second, then rolled his eyes and told her to get out of the chair. Afterward, she watched as he lavished attention on another comic, a beautiful brunette ex-model with Caucasian features that he was probably more accustomed to making up. Cho took solace in the fact that she was the funnier of the two, but it brought back those old pangs that she'd never fulfill society's definition of "pretty."

Margaret Cho, Television Star

In 1992, Cho moved to Los Angeles and into a house with several other young performers. Between road gigs, she auditioned for TV and movie parts. In this town full of beautiful people, however, her insecurity about her looks and her weight began to really depress her. "I felt sexless, useless, ugly, and fat," she wrote, "and had no idea how I was going to get past my physical self and show the producers that I actually had a lot of talent." She was persistent, though, and went to audition after audition.

Cho found it difficult to get an agent. Before she found one, she received many rejections, some of which had everything to do with her race and nothing to do with her talent. One agent from a major agency said he wouldn't represent her because it was too hard for Asian people to make it in show business. His proof? He'd once had a Chinese client who couldn't get any jobs, and he didn't want to go through that again. Finally, Cho caught a break and found an agent named Karen Taussig, who took her on and booked her gigs around the country, including many at college campuses.

Soon Cho was traveling so much that she began to feel like a traveling salesperson, eating dinner out of vending machines and getting lost on snowy, icy roads in rural areas. She ended up in small towns, where people would see her Asian features and assume she could not speak English. She visited so many places in so short a time that she began to wake up with no idea where she was. She would open the drawer in the nightstand and check the phone book. She would go days without talking to anyone, except to her audience during the show. She even celebrated her birthday alone in a gas station restaurant. "I went to hell and back in the name of comedy," she wrote.

Even at home in Los Angeles, she couldn't escape the road. She would wake up in the middle of the night from a nightmare that she had missed a flight. She would jump out of bed, gather her clothes into a suitcase, get dressed, and then realize that it was her day off. Cho was miserable, but thanks to Taussig, she began to play bigger and better venues on the road. She became the most booked act in the college circuit and garnered a nomination for Campus Comedian of the Year.

The title earned her appearances on a late-night TV show hosted by Arsenio Hall, as well as on a prime-time "Young Comedians" special hosted by Bob Hope. In addition, when Karen felt that Cho had had enough experience to hone her act, she set up showcases in Los Angeles so Cho could perform for network executives. The showcases sparked a bidding war among the major studios, and in the end, Cho got an amazing deal. It was every stand-up comedian's dream—a ticket out of the land of endless road gigs, nights spent in musty motels in strange cities, and constant rejections after auditions. Margaret Cho was going to be the star of her very own sitcom.

This was amazing to Cho, probably because she had been such a TV addict as a kid. During periods of isolation and loneliness, TV had been her friend. She chose to work with ABC,

ASIAN AMERICANS ON TV

Cho frequently laments the lack of Asian Americans on TV and in movies. "Don't call me about your script," she tells all writers and producers. "I know it's going to be one of *those* parts [a liquor store owner, a purveyor of exotic mushrooms and ginseng, an exchange student, etc.], and I don't have time to be reminded once again that my story is never going to be told by anyone but me." *All-American Girl* premiered in the 1990s, and that was the first sitcom about an Asian-American family. Think of how many sitcoms exist about white families.

Now think of your favorite TV shows or even TV shows you have seen only once or twice. How many have regular Asian characters? Are they stereotypical, or do they seem more complex, more three-dimensional? (Can you tell, based on stereotypes alone, that they are supposed to be Asian?) Once you begin to notice how many Asian Americans are represented on television, you will likely notice that there are not too many, and many of those shown are representing a stereotype. Asian characters appeared in these programs, from the past and present:

- *Sanford and Son* (1974–1976; Pat Morita played Ah Chew, Sanford's friend.)
- *Happy Days* (1975–1982; Pat Morita played Matsuo "Arnold" Takahashi, a diner owner.)
- *Ally McBeal* (1998–2001; Lucy Liu is Ling Woo, a ruthless lawyer.)
- *The Gilmore Girls* (2000–; Keiko Agena is Lane Kim, the rebellious daughter of a conservative Korean mother.)
- *Entourage* (2005–; Rex Lee is Lloyd, Ari Gold's eccentric, capable assistant.)
- *Lost* (2004–; Daniel Dae Kim plays Jin Kwon.)
- *Grey's Anatomy* (2005–; Sandra Oh plays hard-driving surgical intern Cristina Yang.)

because that was the network that aired the shows she loved best—*Fantasy Island, Charlie's Angels, The Love Boat,* and *Battle of the Network Stars.* ABC had a good track record in producing sitcoms centered around strong female comics, including *Roseanne* (Roseanne Barr), *Ellen* (Ellen DeGeneres) and *Grace Under Fire* (Brett Butler). When she went to meet with the executives at the network, they said they wanted to produce a sitcom that revolved around the life of an Asian-American family. At that point, Cho gave little thought to the content of the show—she was just looking forward to being a superstar and to having lots of adoring fans, to being chauffeured around in a limousine, and all the other perks that came with fame. "The network deal made me think my life had been saved," she wrote. "I had paid my dues—and then some. . . . I looked at a future so bright, I had to wear shades."

Life certainly did get exciting for Cho. Suddenly, she had a publicist who was driving her to photo shoots and interviews. People wanted to see what she looked like and know what she was thinking. She had meetings with TV writers who were auditioning for the chance to write her show. Because the show was based on Cho's life, the writer they finally hired fashioned the pilot episode from her answers to his questions about her upbringing, her childhood, her thoughts, and her dreams. He combined this material with material from her stand-up comedy act, which was also very much about being a second-generation Asian American.

The pilot he ended up writing was somewhat based on Cho's life. For instance, the part of her character's little brother was inspired by Cho's real-life brother, Hahn. Like Hahn, the brother was pulled in two directions: On one hand, he wanted to be a dutiful son, but he also looked up to his rebellious sister. Mostly, though, the show was pure fiction, and the characters were one-dimensional stereotypes—the conservative mother obsessed with marrying off her daughter; the submissive but wise father (played by Clyde Kusatsu); and the overachieving,

Margaret Cho and B.D. Wong, the costar of her sitcom *All-American Girl*, arrive at the second annual Comedy Hall of Fame.

dutiful older brother, (played by B.D. Wong). There was also the conflicted younger brother and the live-in grandmother with a heavy accent and a twinkle in her eye (played by Amy Hill). Cho played the role of Margaret Kim, a rebellious daughter living in this typically conservative Korean-American household. Margaret Kim was not a stand-up comedian—she went to college and worked at a department store cosmetics counter.

This was the first time an Asian-American family would be featured in a sitcom, and the program would air at 8:00 P.M., when children would be watching. Therefore, the storylines were kept wholesome. They skipped over Cho's problems with drugs and alcohol in high school. Instead, the character rebelled by wearing short miniskirts and by dating boys who were not Korean. In the pilot, her character performs a stand-up comedy act that embarrasses her family, and at the end of the episode, she vows never to publicly embarrass her family again.

All went well until Cho had a screen test. When she returned home, she got a call from the producer, Gail, who was very upset. Gail was the head of the company producing the show for ABC. She and Cho had grown close during the development stages of the show, but when she called, there was none of the usual friendliness in her voice. Cho wrote in her memoir that she will never forget the words that Gail spoke that evening:

> We need to do something . . . I have to tell you. . . . The network has a problem with you. They are concerned about the fullness of your face. You need to lose weight. I don't care what you do. We have two weeks before we shoot the pilot. I am so sorry but there isn't any way to make this nice. And far be it from me to say anything. . . . But this is for you, for your future. If you want your own show, if you want to be a star, you'll do it.

Cho could not get past the fact that they had singled out her face. How do you change your face? It is the only body part you cannot change, but if she did not find a way to do so, she would not be a star. "I felt like the Elephant Man," she wrote. She spoke to her agent, Karen Taussig, who wanted to pull her from the show. Karen read Gail's request as a sign that this was the wrong project for Cho. All Cho knew, though, was that she did not want to go back on the road. She had to make this work. So she fired Karen and hired a new agent. Meanwhile, ABC rallied to get Cho on a diet-and-exercise regimen to take off the pounds quickly. They hired a personal trainer to come to her house at 7 A.M. for four hours, six mornings a week. They hired a company to deliver food to her house—tiny portions of healthy, low-fat food. She dreamt about the foods she was once allowed to eat, and when she was hungry, she drank water.

The trainer and new diet worked, because she lost a lot of weight in a dangerously brief period of time. The network resumed rehearsals for the show, which now had a name: *All-American Girl*. Cho had lost 30 pounds in two weeks, and she became very sick. In her trailer one day, she went to the bathroom and urinated blood. In the hospital, they discovered that her kidney was failing. She was bleeding internally. Still, she kept quiet, because she wanted nothing to interfere with her dieting. She feared that if she went off her diet, they might stop production on the show.

To help keep the weight off, Cho turned to even more unhealthy methods. The show's costume designer told her about a doctor who prescribed diet pills. She began taking pills as well as laxatives. All of this made her feel even sicker—she had migraines and panic attacks, and it hurt to urinate.

This pressure to lose weight was a familiar one. Cho had been hearing it all her life. When her parents phoned, they sometimes greeted her with "How is your weight?" instead of "hello." When she was eight, her father told her after a ballet recital that she was the fattest ballerina (she never went back to ballet class). Cho's mother had an eating disorder,

ASIAN AMERICANS IN HOLLYWOOD

It is possible that because Margaret Cho began to watch television at such a young age, she became aware very early that Asian Americans were portrayed infrequently on screen. One of her most often-repeated jokes is from *Notorious C.H.O.,* when she admits that when she was little, she would dream about one day appearing as an extra on the TV show, *MASH.* Of course, playing an extra on a show about a medical unit stationed in Korea during the Korean War is a pretty measly dream—and that was the joke. If an Asian-American kid wants to grow up to be a movie star, the best he or she can hope for is to play an extra. Another of Cho's jokes is that when she was watching *Kung Fu*, starring David Carradine, she would think to herself that the name of the show should be, "This Guy Isn't Asian!"

In her blog, in October 2005, Cho wrote:

It is weird being Asian American right now, because I don't exactly know what my place is. America is supposed to be for everyone, and people are supposed to treat me like I belong here, and yet you would never know that from watching TV or movies. I still get the questions about where I am really from. Then when I try to explain this feeling of invisibility to those whose every move and moment is entirely visible, they come back at me with, "Maybe Asian Americans don't want to be in entertainment!" Yes, he really said that. I just screamed, because there was no other way I could answer without hitting him.

Cho knows firsthand from her own experience that Asian Americans certainly want to be in entertainment. She laments that the situation now is no different than it was in Hollywood in the first half of the twentieth century, when significant Asian parts were frequently played by heavily made-up Caucasian actors. A former writer for *All-American Girl* wrote a play about a Chinese-American actress, Anna May Wong, who worked in Hollywood during this period. Wong became very hopeful when she was brought into the studio to test extensively for the part of O-lan in the film adaptation of Pearl Buck's novel *The Good Earth*. The part ended up going to a

German actress, Luise Rainer, who won an Oscar for the role in 1937. Wong was devastated.

This playwright asked Cho to read the part of Wong during a public reading of the play in Los Angeles in 2004. Reading the part of Wong, Cho was reminded anew that things are not really so much different now than they were almost a century ago. Parts for Asian Americans are still largely limited to martial artists, massage parlor denizens, and opium addicts. In fact, the 2005 *New York Times* obituary for actor Pat Morita calls him "one of the last survivors of a generation of Asian-American actors who toiled within a system that was only interested in the stock Asian." Then the obit writer points out a 2004 movie, *50 First Dates*, in which a white actor played the part of a stock Asian, the leering Hawaiian. Where is the evidence that anything has changed for the better?

Cho feels that this blatant disregard for a group of people who make up such a large part of the country's population is just plain wrong. She tries to use her fame as a platform to draw attention to these types of imbalances. She was not always this way. When she was a teenager, Cho actively avoided the Asian-American kids on her campus who were earnestly handing out fliers advertising Asian Student Union meetings. They embarrassed her. Similarly, early in her career, when she was invited to participate in a comedy special featuring political comedians, she declined.

Cho realized later that because she was an Asian-American woman who talked publicly about race and equal rights, she already was political. It was something she could not deny. "I know better now," she wrote in her blog on October 4, 2004. "And it is immensely pleasing when I am referred to as a political comedian, because it feels true. It feels strong." Cho's life lies in stark contrast to that of her parents: They have lived in America since 1964 and have never once voted in an election. "When I ask them why, they simply say, 'We aren't supposed to.' . . . I guess [my father] doesn't want to explain, because how can you explain something as intangible as invisibility?"

B.D. Wong also accompanied Margaret Cho to the Emmy Awards in 1994.

and she had many cousins and other distant relations who were anorexic.

The comments Cho's family made about her weight only added to the pressure being applied by the TV studio. One of her uncles saw her on TV and called her mother immediately to suggest a diet for Margaret—it consisted of eating one small bag of rice per week. You made the rice last all week by chewing each bite 50 times. He also sent the "diet" to Cho in the mail and faxed it, then followed up the letter and fax with a phone call. No one in Cho's family ever told her that she was beautiful just the way she was. Instead, she heard over and over again that she was too big. Looking back later in her life, Cho saw that all of this focus on her weight while she was growing up made the network's comments even more effective at driving her into a weight-loss frenzy, even at the expense of her health.

The media just made matters worse. They picked up immediately on the fact that Cho was not thin. "Cho, who is not svelte," wrote one critic; "Beauty is not Cho's strong point," wrote another. One tabloid ran the headline "Margaret Cho Has Thunder Thighs," and *Star* magazine published a "Chow like Cho" diet. No one focused on the talent that had made Cho such a huge success on the college stand-up circuit. Everyone focused on her looks.

Still, in 1994, the network picked up 13 episodes of *All-American Girl*, and Cho was ecstatic. She flew to New York, where they were airing the pilot for the executives, to wait for the news. Like a true rising star, she stayed at a posh hotel and shopped at expensive stores. She was in her hotel room when the phone rang and she heard the good news. She and a friend jumped up and down and ordered room service. People sent champagne and flowers. The phone was ringing off the hook. Finally, her parents were proud.

Imagine what it is like to walk down the red carpet and hear the paparazzi calling your name, calling for you to turn toward them for a picture. This is what happened at a party in Los

Margaret Cho arrives at the American Comedy Awards in 1995, the year before she won an award for the Funniest Female Stand-up Comedian.

Angeles after the network made the announcement about the production of *All-American Girl*. Cho felt like a star. In addition, she was getting used to hobnobbing with other stars, such as Teri Hatcher and Ellen DeGeneres, at these parties. The industry was abuzz about her show, the first Asian-American family sitcom. The premiere got huge ratings—everyone wanted to see what the buzz was all about.

Unfortunately, neither the TV critics nor the Asian-American community took kindly to the show. Critics lamented that the show was too blah. "Instead of exploring or even exploiting the Korean-ness of the situation, *All-American Girl* relies on variations of old gags," wrote the *Boston Globe*. Other articles claimed that Cho was having a negative impact on the Korean community. One leader in the Korean-American community called Cho "dangerous," saying that the show needed to be monitored. A 12-year-old girl wrote a letter to the editorial section of a San Francisco newspaper that said, "When I see Margaret Cho on television, I feel deep shame." Cho was devastated and angered by this reaction from her own community. She took the negative reactions very personally.

Ratings dropped week after week. The network went to desperate measures to fix the show. They hired an Asian consultant to try and make it more "authentic." She chased Cho around with chopsticks, gave the cast origami lessons, and taught them how to use an abacus. "The idea that there is one defining, 'authentic' Asian-American experience," wrote Cho, "ignores the vast diversity of which we are capable. It discounts the fact that there can be many truths." The network did not see this. They only wanted one stereotypical truth. They continued to strategize and re-tool, changing the focus from family life to Cho's life—her character moved into the basement of the house and then into an apartment with two roommates.

Then they shot a new pilot with all new actors except for Cho and the woman who had played her grandma in the original show. In the new version, she lived in an apartment with

Margaret Cho was on hand for Drew Carey's roast at the New York Friars Club in 1998. Carey's show replaced *All-American Girl*.

three male roommates. It fell flat, and in the spring of 1995 the show was canceled. No one even called Cho to tell her the show was canceled. When she did find out, though, she also learned that it was being replaced by the *Drew Carey Show*, which starred Carey, an overweight male comic. Of course, it is very unlikely that anyone asked Carey to lose weight for his show. Cho later commented that this was a prime example of how differently society treats men and women. "It's not acknowledged as unfair," she said, "and it should be."

Bouncing Back

Cho took the demise of *All-American Girl* hard, and personally. "I was 23 years old, and I just wanted to have people like me for once," she said. She was deeply depressed, and she escaped to New York, then to Europe with a friend. She drowned her misery in alcohol and in bad relationships. Later, looking back on the show, she said, "There were just so many people involved . . . and so much importance put on the fact that it was an ethnic show. . . . Then, for fear of being too 'ethnic,' it got so watered down for television that by the end, it was completely lacking in the essence of what I am and what I do."

She felt like her world was falling apart. She had focused all her hopes and dreams on the show, then it failed. Her self-esteem sank along with it. She hit rock bottom, and she realized one night that something had to change. In her stand-up comedy act, she talks about that night, about waking up one morning and realizing she had been so drunk that she hadn't even noticed that she had wet her bed. "I said, what kind of Motley Crue, 'Behind the Music,' lifestyle is this?" she wrote. "I realized it's not me. And it just really struck me as very stupid. So I just kind of woke up."

Cho rebuilt her confidence slowly and surely. She began doing stand-up while sober, and she realized all over again that she

IMPRESSIONS OF MOM

The one thread that runs through all of Cho's comedy, from her earliest performances at the Rose & Thistle to her most recent show, is the impressions she does of her mom. It is an instant crowd-pleaser—the room explodes in thunderous applause once Cho begins an impression. She might as well be a top-40 artist playing her most requested hit. She started doing the impressions when she was growing up:

> I think that when you're a child of immigrants, your parents are very embarrassing to you. And, you know, you kind of can't really deal with it, you know? I would get really embarrassed by my mom, because she wasn't American. To me, she was a foreigner. And so I was always doing her accent to my friends, always making fun of her, because getting that laughter, getting that approval from other people made me feel better about who I was. And that embarrassment over her accent . . . when I could do the impression of her in front of my friends, it made it all better.

For example, Cho's mom could not pronounce the name "Montgomery Ward." When she said it, it came out more like "Mommary Waaar."

Cho was worried at first about her mother's reaction to seeing her impressions, but her mom did not mind. By the time Young Hie Cho went to see Margaret perform, her daughter was popular enough to be playing a major venue that was packed with enthusiastic fans. These fans considered Cho's mother a minor celebrity. Cho jokes about being worried about her mother's reaction to her show, only to find her mother milling around in the lobby, basking in the attention.

loved being on stage and making people laugh. She began doing yoga, she adopted a dog, and she broke up with a boyfriend who was not good for her. She got back together with Karen Taussig, the agent who had advised her to walk away from ABC when she was told to lose weight. It was easy to break the contract with her current agent, a guy who had once told her, "The Asian thing puts people off." Once again, Karen booked her at clubs and colleges, as she had before Cho began to work with the TV network. "I realized that when I was onstage with the mike, I was home, and that when I am at peak performance, when the crowd is right, the night is relatively young, and God is there, nobody does it better."

Cho recorded a new comedy CD and donated the proceeds to an AIDS clinic in Houston. Karen and a friend traveled with her this time, so she didn't feel so lonely on the road. She also appeared in the movie *It's My Party*. She played a close friend of the main character, Nick, a young gay man who decides to throw himself one last hurrah after his AIDS symptoms become life-threatening. Newly sober and enjoying her work for the first time in a long time, Cho felt refreshed. She began to write material about her experience doing *All-American Girl*. Once she began talking about it, she felt all of the built-up misery and despair fade away. All of a sudden, the whole episode seemed hilariously horrendous. By talking about it, maybe she could help others who were going through similar battles with their weight and self-esteem. A lot of people feel like outsiders. A lot of people suffer from low self-esteem. Her experience, Cho realized, was nothing to be ashamed of, and it was universal. Maybe by presenting it through the prism of comedy, with her own brand of brash humor, she could show people that they are not alone and that they can overcome it, too. It was healing for her and for her audiences.

This period in Cho's life led to the show (and book of the same name) *I'm the One That I Want*. In June 1999, the one-woman show opened off-Broadway, and it was extremely well

Cho brought her off-Broadway one-woman show *I'm the One That I Want* to a packed house in York, Pennsylvania, in 1999.

Cho has turned her show *I'm the One That I Want* into a revealing and honest biography that focuses on her eventual self-acceptance.

received. The show is about the importance of loving yourself so that you do not have to depend on everyone else to love you. In it, Cho condemns, among other things, plastic surgery and

The women from the popular comedy variety show *SCTV* were an inspiration to Margaret Cho. The cast reunited at the U.S. Comedy Arts Festival in 1999. Front row from left are: Dave Thomas, Catherine O'Hara, Andrea Martin, Eugene Levy, and Martin Short. In the back row are Joe Flaherty, *(left)*, and Harold Ramis *(right)*.

the growing numbers of Asian women seeking nose elongations and eye-widening operations to look more Caucasian.

During this time, Cho finally let go of her own obsession with being thin. She likens the process to winning a war. She made her own experience into a manifesto: "We need to stop taking exercise classes named 'Butt Burners' and 'Saddlebags 101.' We have to stop buying magazines that scream on the cover, 'Get the body you want now!' We have to stop living our lives with dressing on the side." At the same time, she was living what she spoke. Instead of buying "skinny" clothes that she might be able to wear in a few months, she started buying clothes that fit her. Instead of starving herself and exercising excessively, she began eating what she wanted and she discovered exercise that she actually liked, including yoga and, later, belly dancing.

She took the show on a 40-city tour, and it sold out in every venue. A feature film was made of a live recording of the show, at the Warfield in San Francisco. Cho and her longtime agent, Karen Taussig, formed their own production company, Cho Taussig Productions, so no one else could come along and threaten Cho with any kind of ultimatum. Finally, after working since age 16, she was 31 years old and she was fully in charge of her career.

The film garnered incredible reviews and broke the record for the most money grossed per print in movie history. Her book became a bestseller. She ended the book with a story about a gay couple, Yutaka and Ti, whom she had met at a show in Hawaii. One of the men was very sick. He was dying from AIDS. His boyfriend came to see Cho later, after the sick man had died, and told her that when his boyfriend was suffering and in the hospital, he listened to the CD of her show and that kept his spirits high. "Whatever success I have had," she wrote, "that is the single one that I am most proud of."

Patron Saint of Outsiders

After the success of her first show, Cho was swimming in accolades. In 2000, the Gay and Lesbian Alliance Against Defamation (GLAAD) awarded her their first Golden Gate Award. The organization's spokesperson named the following reasons for giving Cho the award:

> Comedian and actress Margaret Cho—who has struggled herself to bridge and transcend cultural barriers—has celebrated and affirmed the lesbian, gay, bisexual and transgender community's diversity. From her routine inclusion of lesbian and gay themes in her routines—most notably in her 2000 Media Award–nominated show *I'm the One That I Want*—to her role as the close friend of an openly gay man with AIDS in *It's My Party* to her benefit performances on behalf of AIDS and lesbian and gay community organizations, Cho has been among the community's strongest allies. GLAAD is proud to present her with its first-ever Golden Gate Award, honoring

a member of the entertainment or media community who, as a pioneer, has made a significant difference in promoting equal rights for all, regardless of sexual orientation or gender identity.

She followed it up with a new show, *Notorious C.H.O.*, in 2001, and went on a smash-hit 37-city national tour that culminated in a sold-out concert at Carnegie Hall in New York City. The name *Notorious C.H.O.* was inspired by the women of rap—Missy Elliot, Eve, Lil' Kim—who Cho believed were heading up the fourth wave of feminism, or the latest generation of feminists, some of whom are characterized by their disregard for the old notion that drawing attention to one's sexuality will undercut a woman's credibility and power. The show, recorded and released as a feature film, was hailed by the *New York Times* as "Brilliant!" The concert material was raunchy, and it dealt mostly with her struggles with body image, sexual identity, and ethnic stereotyping. Watching her perform, she makes it look easy, but later, she wrote about the difficulty not only of being a minority, but of breaking down that experience so that it is relatable to the public:

> There is definitely something to be said for having aspects of minority life illuminated so you can thoughtfully examine your own culture and feel lucky to be who you are. Discussing a heritage and having a collective past that is oppressed and depressing can be a lovely way to spend time after dinner on the front porch as the sun goes down. Friendships can be built on a legacy of loathing, and how wonderful some of the bonds forged in this repressive world can be. But sometimes, I just really get sick of fighting all the time. I am doing battle when I am sleeping. I have to slay the dragons of the myth of heterosexual European male society in my

Margaret Cho has always been a supporter of gay rights. Here she performs the opening monologue at the 16th annual GLAAD Media Awards in 2005.

dreams, then get up in the morning and be an activist. I have to watch movies and news about the people that I am not, then I have to translate all of my difficulties and observations in order to make my struggle palatable to those who don't have to march, but are sympathetic to my voice. . . .

What if there really was a level playing field? . . . Wouldn't I really be able to fly then?

I have posed this question to other minority artists, and get stumped by answers like "No, not ever have I ever wanted to be white." And I just don't buy it. Why would you not want things to be easier?

In a review of *Notorious C.H.O.*, the *Washington Post* called Cho the "patron saint of anyone who has ever felt like an outsider." It was an apropos observation, as her confessional comedy attracted a cult-like following of anyone and everyone who had ever felt like an outsider—and this, as it turned out, was an enormous group. You could see them crowding her gigs and hear them shouting messages of love to her from the audience. In her concert films, the camera panned the crowd waiting outside the venue. "I'm so excited that there are fans lined up around the block," Cho said on the DVD commentary for *Notorious C.H.O.*, "and I hope I can always deliver that expectation, that kind of adrenaline that happens when you go see a performer. I really respect that energy, I respect it a lot because I know what it takes to actually go and buy a ticket." The people streaming into the theater take some time to testify to the camera about the important role Cho plays in their lives. "Margaret Cho is one of my saviors," said one concertgoer. "I'm 15, and I came out when I was 13, and I never knew that somebody as young as 13 could be openly gay with his friends, with his family. I didn't know there were people who supported that until I found Margaret Cho."

Cho's parents came to see *Notorious C.H.O.* when it was at Davies Symphony Hall, in San Francisco. Their pride was obvious. During the show, Cho introduced them, and they stood up and waved to everyone. Her dad held up a World Cup Korea towel, because Korea had just hosted the World Cup. "I was so embarrassed," Cho said.

In an interview with her parents at the beginning of the movie, Cho's mom reported, "I went to the restroom this evening, and I said, 'Hi. I'm Margaret's mother. I'm so happy. Thanks

MEMBERS OF CHO'S CLASS

As Cho was growing up, she found few minority comedians to look up to. Today, a good number of African-American, Hispanic, and female comedians act as role models for the current generation of budding stand-up comedians, there are still very few Asian-American comedians. Cho jokes that on a recent book tour, people kept asking her what it was like to star in *Charlie's Angels*—they mistook her for one of the only other Asian women in showbiz, Lucy Liu.

Cho explains the void this way: "Korean culture holds onto these things like, 'Don't make waves' or 'Don't cause a fuss,'—because if you argue about something being racist, it's embarrassing because it sort of implies that you are offended. And to be offended is kind of a bad idea, because it means that you are vulnerable to something." She holds out hope for the future, however, and meanwhile lauds the following fellow comedians for using comedy as a tool to open up discussion about what it is like to be a minority in America. They subscribe to her statement, "Life is a tragedy for those who feel and a comedy for those who think."

Dave Chapelle was born in 1973 in Washington, D.C., and grew up in Ohio, Maryland, and Washington, D.C. He was inspired by Richard Pryor to become a comedian, and at age 14, he went onstage for the first time at the Apollo Theater in for coming to see my daughter. Thank you.' I really expressed myself. I said, 'It's a miracle.'"

The director of the movie cut back and forth between Cho and her parents. Cho said, "I can't believe my mother was in the bathroom thanking people before the show—that is so her, though, she is so gracious. When she sees people standing in line, she wants to go up and thank them for coming."

Harlem, in Upper Manhattan. He was booed offstage, but the experience did not discourage him. Chappelle attended a high school for the performing arts in Maryland and honed his skills there. In the 1980s, he broke into TV on *Russell Simmons' Def Comedy Jam*. He landed his own show on Comedy Central, *Chappelle's Show*, which became known for its smart social and political commentary.

Comedian George Lopez was born in 1961 and grew up near Los Angeles in the Mission Hills of the San Fernando Valley. He first became popular in the Latino community for his satirizing of Mexican-American life and culture in the United States. He also draws material from his upbringing, which was defined by financial poverty and bedwetting due to a genetic defect that caused his kidneys to malfunction. (His family made fun of him instead of bringing him to the doctor.) Lopez has released four comedy albums, and stars in his own sitcom on ABC, the *George Lopez Show*.

Sandra Bernhard was born in 1955 in Flint, Michigan. She is an actress, singer and comedian, but she got her start in showbiz doing outrageous stand-up comedy defined by its outspokenness about celebrity culture, political figures, her bisexuality, women's rights, bigotry, and just about every other hot-button issue. Bernhard has written and performed two one-woman shows, *Without You I'm Nothing* and *Everything Bad & Beautiful*.

She said, "It was really surreal to have my parents in the audience because this show is so incredibly 'outlaw' in its overt sexuality, in its political nature, that there is so much maturity in the show. I wasn't sure if my parents were ready to see me as such an adult." Cho's mother told her afterward that she was so nervous during the show that she was holding tightly onto the arms of her chair. Cho laughed, "I'm not a rollercoaster. Why were you holding on so tight?"

Think about what Cho's parents went through, though—from their daughter not fitting into the mold of "nice Korean girl," to her getting expelled from high school and not going to college, to choosing a career that they were sure was a formula for failure. Parenting Margaret Cho must have been similar to riding a rollercoaster! As for listening to her mature material, Cho once told an interviewer, "A Korean reporter once asked me—he said, 'Do your Korean parents feel ashamed that their daughter, their Korean daughter, is onstage talking about the things you talk about?' And I said, 'I don't think they're ashamed because they're Korean. I think any parents would be ashamed.'"

In the interview during *Notorious C.H.O.*, Cho's father said, "It's embarrassing listening to her joke in some sense because she's talking about sexual matters, which you do not talk about in front of your children or in front of your parents. But on the other hand, this is a matter that is so close to all of us, right? There's something to think about, something to be laughed at, right?" He looked at his wife. She replied, "Right. Right."

Later in the interview, Cho's father said, "I feel that my decision to live in this country was the right decision. There are many reasons, but most of all, [Margaret] has a platform to tell her stories to everybody, and she's doing so well." It makes one wonder whether Cho's material would have gone over so well in South Korea. What would her material be like if she had grown up there? Cho is happy to have grown up in the United States. Her *Notorious C.H.O.* tour launched right after the terrorist attacks of September, 11, 2001. In the beginning of that concert film, Cho told the audience, "No matter what the terrorists do, I refuse to be terrorized. They can't take away my security, my peace of mind, my freedom. I am an American."

Still, Cho's defining experiences as an American are the ones that remind her that she is perceived as an outsider in this society. She explained during a radio interview all the different ways she had felt like an outsider in her life:

> In my family, even in the Korean community in general, I was always a bit too loud, a bit too awkward, a bit too fat, a bit too clumsy. I was never a delicate flower, as most of the women in my family were. And so I'd always felt kind of out of place, and I never really had friends in school. I never really had a clique to run with. I was never cool. And I think that when you spend most of your life not being cool, at some point, you just don't care anymore. And I sort of let go of the idea of being cool and let go of the idea of being accepted, and I think that's what really gave me the ability to be an artist.

Her outsider status fed her stand-up material. If she was not an outsider, she never would have noticed how annoying it was when people asked her where she was from.

"San Francisco," she would answer.

They would inevitably say, "No, where are you really from?" They wanted to know which country in Asia and once they found out, they wanted to tell her which kinds of Korean foods they favored.

"I just don't get it," Cho said. "I don't go up to white people and say, 'Hey, are you from France? I mean not recently, but a couple of hundred years ago. I thought so! I love your fries.' " These are the types of everyday observations that she has brought to her comedy. They are funny and profound. They strike a chord. They make people in the audience think twice the next time they want to ask an Asian American where she is

Cho, with musician Darius Rucker and famous drag queen Lady Bunny, attends the WEDrock Concert For Freedom To Marry in New York City.

from. For those in the audience who have been in Cho's shoes, the observation confirmed that they were not alone. "It's very moving to see so many different people in my audience," she said. "I feel like I really identify with them, too, and we get a lot of comfort from each other."

In another show, she mentions that people who know she's Korean will bring up the fact that North Korea is making nuclear weapons. They will say to her, "Well? What's going on?"

"Like my uncle's making 'em!" she said. "Yeah, I'll just call him up."

"I have them right here," she said, pretending to be her uncle, in Korea, speaking in broken English. "I have one, two, three, four, five—how many you need?"

Once she started her Weblog in 2003, she could share more of these types of observations with her fans, and she did, posting regularly to her site http://www.margaretcho.com:

> Yesterday I did a giant round of radio interviews, and some of these people are not sure what to make of me. One guy was keen to talk about race. . . . He said, "Asian girls are hot!!" I said, "That is nice. So that is the only contribution we make to society?" "Yeah! They are hot!!" Wow. We have been the leaders in science and medicine, made great strides in art and culture. We invented pasta.
>
> But all that he can come up with is that we are hot. I am not denying that we are hot. It is just that—well, that is very sad.

In 2003, at age 34, Cho married Al Ridenour at their home in Glendale, California, the same town where she used to visit her cousins as a teenager and sit by the pool reading *Teen Beat*. It was Ridenour's third time walking down the aisle. It was Cho's first, but she was surprised it was actually happening. "I got very used to the delicious dream of spinsterhood, independence in solitude, gardening and animal rescue, a varied and lengthy succession of lovers, rejection of the Cinderella fantasies of my peers." She had seen most of her friends already go through one or two divorces, and she figured she would never follow them down the aisle. She asks:

> So why am I getting married? Because somebody I love asked me, and I want to. I know I am already complete, because I've had to fight to realize my completeness, to see it when all I was offered was blindness. So now that I have seen it, I just want to spend all my parents' money and have an embarrassing semi-Satanic wedding where, instead of wedding vows, we exchange blood.

Ridenour is an artist, actor, writer, and longtime pied piper of L.A.'s counterculture. He spent most of his teens and early 20s in Indiana, attending Indiana University, where he majored in English and German literature. He arrived in California from the Midwest in 1989, to study film at UCLA (University of California–Los Angeles). Ridenour is most well known for his performance art. Soon after his arrival in L.A., he became involved with the L.A. Cacophony Society, which is defined on its Web site as "an open network of creative dissidents, artists, seekers, and radical pilgrims" and in a newspaper article as "a social group for the antisocial: those who prefer to think of themselves as outcasts." Ridenour joined because he was interested in the art scene, but, as he told a reporter, "I longed to be involved with something besides going to art openings and clubs."

The Cacophony Society is very different from the usual art openings and clubs. According to *L.A. Weekly*, each month the group organizes a series of activities "that get them out of the dank corners of boho enclaves like coffeehouses and underground night-clubs and into smudgy and pleasingly confusing worlds of their own making." These activities are impromptu performances in public spaces, seemingly designed to confuse, alarm, and make audience members out of bystanders who certainly did not expect to see a show. Once, they walked down Hollywood Boulevard picking up every available piece of litter and gluing it onto their clothing. Another time, they marketed their own line of teddy bears called the Cement Cuddlers. They smuggled the very heavy toys onto the shelves at Toys "R" Us, then pretended to be frenzied customers. They inquired about price and created a fuss over the bears that mirrored consumers' actual clamoring for popular toys such as Tickle Me Elmo.

These zany "actions" prompt one question: Why? "We do this to entertain, to confuse," Ridenour, who was soon crowned Grand Instigator of the society, explained to one reporter. "There's also a little criticism implied." An article that ran in the *L.A. Weekly* gave another answer:

Members of Cacophony create their own entertainments, diversions and realities by inserting eccentric behavior into everyday environments. When they cover themselves in mud and stroll down Rodeo Drive, stumble through Universal CityWalk dressed like post-apocalyptic zombies, or sell bars of mud on Venice Beach as a phony mud-craft organization, they're obviously in it for the pure spectacle. But in their own ridiculous way, they're saying something about how segments of society alienate each other. We are the outcasts, Cacophonists cry out; but look at you—you don't fit in either. Who would want to?

The Cacophony Society has branches in different cities. They devised an annual festival as a gathering for all of their scattered "tribes": Over Labor Day weekend, they would meet in the Black Rock desert, outside Reno, Nevada, and set fire to an effigy, eight-stories tall. This practice evolved into the Burning Man Festival, now an annual weeklong event attended by nearly 25,000 people from all over the world. It is a weeklong party, mixed with a festival of performance art—people dress up in imaginative costumes, spontaneously stage absurdist plays, and meet, mingle, and exchange ideas with like-minded souls.

Since Ridenour left the Cacophony Society in 1999, he has been involved in even more artistic endeavors, including a comedy performance group called "The Art of Bleeding." The group performs a "first-aid education show" based on the teachings of a fictional psychologist named Abram S. Lugner.

Despite the obvious eccentricity of the couple, their home—as it is described in several magazine profiles—sounds ordinarily funky, with bold colors, overstuffed sofas, jewel-toned walls and life-sized Buddha statues in several rooms. In one interview, Cho mentioned that their bedsheets have a thread-count of 1,020—meaning that they are really, really soft and really, really expensive. With such a lush retreat, it is easy to see why

Margaret Cho has made her home in the Hollywood Hills section of Los Angeles a haven from life on the road.

Cho's a self-described homebody—she prefers to be at home with her husband and three dogs to being anywhere else. "[Al's] the perfect caretaker," she said. "He tells me what to eat. If I'm left alone in the house, I'm such a boy. If food's not in front of me, I'll forget to eat. Like I don't know how to go to the store. . . . I'm so used to being in hotels and having room service."

Cho writes her shows and movies at home, and it is hard work. Her stand-up may seem casual and improvisational, but the shows are actually very tightly scripted down to each word and gesture. The timing of every comment and every pause is highly important. It takes her up to a year to hone and fine-tune a new stand-up act. She performs bits and pieces in front of audiences to gauge their reaction, often at smaller clubs around home and in Provincetown, at the tip of Cape Cod in Massachusetts, where she often goes in the summertime.

She embarked on her third sold-out national tour, *Revolution,* in 2003. The tour was heralded as "Her strongest show yet!" by the *Chicago Sun-Times.* The CD of *Revolution* was nominated for a Grammy for best comedy album of the year for 2003. (She lost to George Carlin.) The movie version of the show was filmed at the Wiltern Theater, a historic art deco landmark built in Los Angeles, 1929–1931. The theater has more than 1,000 seats.

Cho described the show as being about "having a revolution within ourselves and within our own lives, and that we are, ourselves, unto ourselves a country. That we can have a constitution, that we can have our own bill of rights we adhere to." The promotional poster was an illustration of Cho wearing a beret similar to the one worn by Communist revolutionary Che Guevara. The reference winked at Cho's stance as the leader of the misfit revolution, as the pied piper of the freak parade. "To me, revolution is the entitlement to change, to empower oneself to change," Cho explained to an interviewer. "That's the most difficult part of revolution—feeling that you deserve one. It is a powerful statement to want one, and of course an even more powerful thing to go about starting one." In the show, she

Cho poses with actress Katy Selverstone, director Lorene Machado, and actor Bruce Daniels at a 2005 screening of the film *Bam Bam and Celeste*.

touched on racism: She told a joke about a flight attendant who is embarrassed to offer her an Asian salad. She also addressed the by-now familiar theme of body image. For speaking so honestly about these important, universal issues—for being a courageous woman—the National Organization for Women gave her an Intrepid Award in July 2003.

In 2004, Cho wrote and starred in a movie, *Bam Bam and Celeste*, which premiered at the Toronto Film Festival in 2005. Cho played Celeste, a 33-year-old woman who, together with her best friend, Bam Bam, played by comedian Bruce Daniels, are still living, so to speak, in the small Midwestern town in which they grew up. Encouraged by a fortune-teller, they embark on a road trip to New York to audition for a reality makeover show. Once they get there, they find that their high-school nemesis is the stylemaker presiding over the show. Not surprisingly, *Bam Bam's* underlying themes have Cho written all over them—during the movie, Celeste learns to become comfortable in her own body and she fights homophobia, racism, and small-town narrow-mindedness.

As Cho performed, she injected more and more political material into her act. She continued to keep the content personal, but now instead of using her personal anecdotes to bring an aspect of society into focus, she targeted the policies of the current U.S. government. "A lot of my comedy before came out of dissatisfaction with my personal life. Now that I'm satisfied, I can look elsewhere for different sources of material," she told an interviewer. She looked to what she considered to be the sad state of the country. In a radio interview in 2004, the host asked why her comedy was socially and politically conscious. Why didn't she just tell jokes without worrying about the state of society? Cho answered, "I think that I have the responsibility to be an activist because of the nature of who I am, as a person of color . . . that this is an opportunity for me to speak my truth and have it be heard and also have it work as entertainment, so anybody who disagrees can enjoy it on a different level. So it's about being of service to the world."

Woman on a Mission

Margaret Cho was very busy in 2004, the year John Kerry challenged incumbent George W. Bush for the U.S. presidency. One of the issues dividing the voters was whether homosexuals should be allowed to marry. Cho campaigned tirelessly for the legalization of same-sex marriage. She folded related material into her shows, and she wrote about it in her Weblog, where she drew parallels to the widespread discrimination against African Americans in the 1950s:

> Gay culture seems to be ever present these days. There are a myriad of television shows: *Queer Eye for the Straight Guy, Boy Meets Boy, Will and Grace, Queer as Folk.* Madonna and Britney practice a little lesbian action on the VMAs. Interior designers are the new rock stars, and gay is the new straight. But there is a co-opting of the culture here, as the mainstream society robs the jewels of queer community, like better window treatments and the importance of a multi-step skincare

Margaret Cho presides over a symbolic mass gay wedding celebration in 2004 in West Hollywood, California.

regimen, but there is still an egregious lack of equality. It seems like gays and lesbians can do all the things that straight people can do, society is saying "You are ok just as you are, just don't try to get married or anything!" It's like when whites stole rock and roll from blacks in the 50s and the kids were all dancing to Little Richard. We love your music, but please don't use that drinking fountain.

In February, when San Francisco governor Gavin Newsom handed out marriage licenses to gay and lesbian couples, Cho appeared on CNBC news to give her opinion on the issue. On Valentine's Day, she appeared at a same-sex marriage held on the steps of the state capitol in Sacramento, California. She dressed as a suffragette, one of the women who agitated for women's voting rights in the early 1900s. She explained her costume to the crowd of 1,000 people by saying that the issue of gay marriage should have been settled back in the early 1900s, that the issue was as old and tired as her outfit. The crowd whooped and hollered when she stepped up to the mike and told the people protesting the rally, people holding signs that read "Polygamy Now" and "Freedom to Marry Dogs" in no uncertain terms that they were not welcome. "We're fighting for the right to be seen as human beings, as loving human beings," she told the crowd. "Don't let them tell you who you might love."

Cho launched www.loveisloveislove.com, a resource site that posts all the legislative goings-on related to the gay-marriage movement. It was her idea to add a page called "Bible Verses," to make the point that Bible verses are not a good foundation for contemporary laws. Cho grew up in a Christian household and attended church regularly as a kid. "I grew up with a lot of Christianity, a lot of spirituality," she said. "God is very important to me, but God doesn't exist for me in the way that's perceived by the Christian right."

Cho's mother grew up as a Buddhist, and even after she converted to Christianity, she never completely abandoned her Buddhist beliefs. The majority of Asia practices either Buddhism or Shinto—the two religions are similar, because they share a basic optimism and a philosophy that all living things are sacred. These ideas were always in the background during Cho's childhood. "A lot of Christianity that came to Asia with the missionaries," she said, "they converted a lot of Korean people to make them born-again Christians and to take away their Shinto beliefs, but they never lost that Shinto. They never lost things like compassion and things like healing the world, like the process of breathing in other people's suffering and breathing out compassion, that meditation, they never really lost that." She thinks all types of religion are beautiful, because they represent a common thread that binds so many disparate groups together. "Here's something people all over the world share, this need for meaning, and how they create meaning out of all the things in their environment is so magical and beautiful," she said.

In her Bible Verses page on www.loveisloveislove.com, she expresses her disappointment in people exploiting the name of the Bible by citing it as justification for their own narrow-mindedness. The page is introduced with this explanation: "The Radical Right likes to justify discrimination against gays and lesbians in our LAW (they say they are only defending their religion, but they're not: they are advocating discrimination in the LAW of the land, not just in their church) by pointing to the Bible. They seem to forget that we don't base our laws on the Bible, and for good reason."

To support this thesis, Cho gives as examples verses that command wives to submit to their husbands as to the Lord; that issue punishment of death to anyone who curses their mother or father; and one that begins, "If a man happens to meet in a town a virgin pledged to be married and he sleeps with her, you shall take both of them to the gate of that town and stone them to death." Her point? The Bible is irrelevant to what is going on in modern times. She also aims to prove that the radical right picks and chooses the verses they want to emphasize. At the bottom of the page are a few that she claims they have overlooked, which include "In everything, do to others what you would have them do to you."

In the 2004 election, Cho wanted John Kerry, the candidate representing the Democrats, to win. His platform was more inclusive of all races, classes, genders, and sexual orientations. In July 2004, Cho was invited to speak at Unity Day, a Human Rights Campaign (HRC) fundraiser scheduled for the first night of the Democratic National Convention in Boston. Because the organizers feared that her comments might cause controversy, however, the invitation was retracted. A spokesperson for the HRC pointed to the firestorm caused by comedian Whoopi

Cho actively campaigned against George Bush during the year of the 2004 elections, including at this performance at "Bush in 30 Seconds Live!" in New York City.

Goldberg's remarks at a fundraiser for John Kerry. Goldberg made sexual puns on the president's name, and this caused Slim-Fast to fire her as its spokeswoman. Some Republicans framed the incident as evidence of Kerry's questionable character and lack of family values. They demanded that the Kerry-Edwards campaign release footage of the rest of the event's speakers. (This did not happen.)

Whoopi responded, "While I can appreciate what the Slim-Fast people need to do in order to protect their business, I must also do what I need to do as an artist, as a writer and as an American—not to mention as a comic. It's unfortunate that, in this country, the two cannot mesh. . . . America's heart and soul is freedom of expression without fear of reprisal." Cho's manager, Karen Taussig, released this statement about Unity Day:

> I am not surprised at the reversal in light of how the Kerry campaign distanced itself from Whoopi's routine in response to the unrelenting media hype and Republican criticism. It's Whoopi's job as a comedian to say things that are sometimes shocking. I wish they could have backed her up. Dennis Miller can make gay jokes about Senators Kerry and Edwards at a recent Bush rally in Wisconsin to a complete absence of media scrutiny. No one demanded a tape of that event or alleged that his comments as a comedian might reflect poorly on Bush.

People were outraged. Petitions were circulated. The National Gay and Lesbian Task Force withdrew its cosponsorship from Unity Day in protest of Cho being uninvited. They released their own press release, announcing, "Throughout her career, Ms. Cho has been a staunch supporter of equal rights for lesbian, gay, bisexual, and transgender (LGBT) Americans, has contributed her time and talent to dozens of LGBT fundraising events, and is much loved by our community. We were proud to recently give her a Task Force Leadership Award. Ms. Cho has said, 'I'm more than bi(sexual).' She is, indeed, one of us. Under these circumstances, we must regretfully withdraw our support for this event."

Cho took the high road, writing in her Weblog, "Although I don't believe it was the right decision, I am not angry with the HRC for withdrawing their invitation for me to perform. I will continue to support them, for we must remain united." She assured her fans that the incident would only make her shout more loudly. As promised, the episode didn't slow her down a bit.

That fall, Cho launched her *State of Emergency* tour, sticking to venues located in some of the election's most contested states. The country was split down the middle, and these "swing states" had the highest numbers of undecided voters. As Election Day grew near, the candidates spent more time campaigning in the swing states instead of wasting time with states that were all but guaranteed to line up behind them. Unfortunately for Cho and others who supported him, Kerry lost.

In September, though, the ACLU honored Cho with their First Amendment Award. Ramona Ripston, executive director of ACLU of Southern California, explained their choice:

> In these very troubled times, when the rights and liberties guaranteed by the Constitution are in jeopardy, we applaud Margaret's courage to speak out about the dangerous policies of the Bush administration and her commitment to organizing others to do the same. More than ever before, this country needs activists and artists like Margaret to stand up and let their voices be heard.

State of Emergency evolved into Cho's fourth show, *Assassin*. Her most political and topical work to date, *Assassin* toured the United States, Canada, and Australia. The movie of the show

In 2005, Cho attended the world premiere of the film *Margaret Cho: Assassin* at the Egyptian Theatre in Hollywood, California.

was filmed in Washington D.C., the seat of the American government against which she railed, at the Warner Theatre. The promotional poster for the tour pictures Cho in a paratrooper costume, holding her microphone as if she is clutching an automatic rifle. The image does homage to the famous 1974 photograph of Patty Hearst, the newspaper heiress who was abducted by an urban guerrilla group called the Symbionese Liberation Army. Hearst surprised everyone by falling in with her captors and assisting them with their illegal activities, including a bank robbery. Cho does not explain the connection to the Patty Hearst image in the show. Maybe she feels that we are all being held hostage, and that our only chance of getting out alive is by staying and fighting. As for the name of the show, she explained, "I wanted to find a name for the show that was the most volatile, provocative, incendiary name, like what would make the right-wing just go kind of crazy? Like, how dare she do this? Who does she think she is?"

In *Assassin*, Cho continued to establish herself as an activist fighting the tide of homophobia, racism, sexism, lookism (discrimination based on appearance), and ethnic stereotyping. "I don't really have anything to lose or gain," she explains. "I don't have any stake in it other than I care about what happens to our country. . . . I care about the way the government and the media and society at large is starting to exclude people slowly, slowly excluding the poor, the minorities, gays, and lesbians. And it

THE FIRST AMENDMENT

On March 31, 1964, comedian Lenny Bruce performed what seemed like an ordinary show at New York City's Café Au Go Go. Bruce was a groundbreaking comedian who had been performing through the 1950s and who, like Cho, was known for pushing the limits of decency—or at least the limits of decency as it is perceived by the mainstream. Bruce riffed on race, sex, religion, and politics, and peppered his act with plenty of swear words. A license inspector in the audience at the March 1964 show counted more than 100. Why was he counting? He planned to submit a report to the district attorney's office, with a recommendation that Bruce be arrested on obscenity charges.

The Supreme Court has ruled many times on obscenity, each time formulating a new definition for what renders material obscene. In 1957, Justice William Brennan penned the majority opinion in *Roth v. the United States*, writing that something was obscene if "to the average person, applying contemporary community standards, the dominant theme of the material as a whole appeals to prurient interest." In 1973, in the judgment for a case called *Miller v. California*, Justice Warren Burger wrote that a work goes farther and farther and farther until it's just these really rich white people and that's it."

These sentiments are echoed in her 2005 book, *I Have Chosen to Stay and Fight*, a collection of essays about some of these same themes, plus love letters to Queen Latifah and Spike Lee and rants about Bill O'Reilly and about limits imposed by the government on women's reproductive rights. One of the essays details a modern affliction she calls "crazy eyes," Cho's own slang for body dysmorphia, a psychiatric disorder characterized by excessive preoccupation with imagined defects in physical appearance, which Cho believes afflicts the majority of women in America. She wrote:

was obscene if an "average person applying contemporary community standards" decides that "the work, taken as a whole, lacks serious literary, artistic, political, or scientific value." Today we are still trying to define "obscene."

As recently as 2004, the Federal Communications Commission was raising tempers by fining radio shock jock Howard Stern for uttering indecencies over the airwaves. Cho has experienced her fair share of censorship, but just like Lenny Bruce, whenever she is censored, she reacts by taking a deep breath and shouting more loudly. "Having the First Amendment means that people like [Cho] can invite trouble," said First Amendment lawyer Ronald Collins, "and that the rest of us will tolerate it. It's to protect ranters, to protect the person who offends us, who gets to us, who challenges our own values."

After a six-month trial, Lenny Bruce was convicted. He appealed, but he died of a drug overdose before the conviction could be overturned. In May 2003, a group of scholars, lawyers, and entertainers, including Margaret Cho, launched a campaign to convince New York Governor George Pataki to grant Bruce a posthumous pardon. Pataki granted it in December of that year.

Margaret Cho teamed up in 2004 with musician-producer-activist Chuck D
to discuss current social and political issues at the UCLA-Hammer Museum
in Los Angeles, California.

Crazy eyes is the ultimate weapon of mass destruction
because it works slowly, eroding the mind and the spirit
and eventually the body, pound by pound, inch by inch,
and it sets its crazy sights upon young women, who provide the gateway to future generations. . . . If crazy eyes
escalated to pandemic proportions, which is the next
level up from the epidemic we have now, there would be
a massive shortage of females capable of reproduction.

This "crazy eyes" analysis is an example of Cho using humor
to link people's experiences to her own and to each other's, and
to use humor to open a discussion about the ridiculous nature
of a serious issue.

Of course, Cho also wrote about gay marriage. "Without the reality of same-sex marriage, there is no freedom," she wrote. Most of the essays from *Stay and Fight* are also posted on her Web site, www.margaretcho.com, as blog entries. Margaret Cho launched her daily Weblog in 2003, and she frequently posts new material. Her blog content runs the gamut from a link to a story about a transgender teen who was banned from attending her high school prom to Cho's latest belly-dancing adventure. "I found that making my thoughts heard online has brought me to an incredible community of other bloggers, who have taken me further into my own quest for truth than anyone could have imagined." Cho is a full believer in the blogger revolution. She even gets her news from blogs instead of from the mainstream media. "I trust the bloggers more than the nightly news, because even though everyone has an agenda, theirs are closer to mine."

8

Healthy Body, Mind, and Soul

"I can't even tell you how beautiful belly-dancing is for someone who's been recovering from anorexia and bulimia for 30 years," said Cho. "One of the things that's so remarkable about belly dance is it frees the belly, it frees the abdomen—and it's really a hard thing to do when you've been holding your stomach in your whole life." She discovered the dance form in 2004 when she attended the Cairo Carnival, an annual event for belly-dancers from all over the world. There she saw scores of women of all different sizes and skin colors dancing with each other and having a great time.

Before she began to study belly dance, Cho had thought it was a dance that women performed for men's entertainment, but she soon realized that it is not for men at all. Belly-dancing is a way for women to celebrate their bodies. "For women to be able to enjoy their bodies is such a gift, it's such an incredible thing," she said, "and I think that's what dance is. That's why I love dance so much." Cho heard about Princess Farhana (Pleasant Gehman), who has been studying, teaching, and writing about

Middle Eastern dance since the early 1990s. She has performed for many Hollywood celebrities and world leaders. Cho went to one of Gehman's classes and immediately loved it. She wrote:

> When you go see a belly dance show, if you look around, a lot of the women are crying. Tears for a million different reasons. Because they can't believe how beautiful the dancer is, and because that beauty is something reachable, accessible, not distant and elusive. Because we have all wasted so many years hating ourselves for how we look and not appreciating ourselves for what we can do. Because we've sucked in our stomachs since we were children and now our backs are racked with pain. Because we have criticized our bodies for so long and we have just begun to feel what it's like to compliment them. Because we have wasted so many years longing for something that didn't really exist, but was sold to us by movies and fashion magazines. Because for many of us, we would have never imagined we could wear something that would expose our midriffs and now that is all we wear! Because bellydancers are never too old, too fat, too ugly, too anything that we are too much of in the "real" world.

Cho declares belly dance to be a place where woman can feel safe. "I'm working hard at freeing myself from these messages I've been fed all my life, from all the negative body images, of all the self-hatred fed to me for years and years from my family, from TV, from magazines," she said. As a means of spreading the karmic wealth, she wrote articles about belly dance, including an essay for *Jane* magazine that explains how belly dance has altered the way she sees herself. "It's like having a new pair of glasses, a rosier, kinder lens that cares more about what I think than what society 'might' think." In belly dance, what is considered chubby by Hollywood standards is considered beautiful.

Margaret Cho's enthusiasm for belly dancing has led to an acceptance of her body, as seen in the outfit she wore to the Grammy Awards in 2004.

It's actually a bonus to have some extra flesh—it makes for better shimmying and undulating.

In spring 2006, Cho began organizing *The Sensuous Woman,* a recurring live revue with a rotating lineup of burlesque, belly dance, and comedy. She performs in the show—her belly-dancing name is her given name, Moran. "This is not just a dance," she said about her newfound obsession. "It's a real remedy for a society that needs change from within. . . . We are allowing ourselves to define our own standard of beauty. . . . There is a path to revolution and ours happens to be paved with glitter and rhinestones."

Cho's sense of revolution and strong stance on controversial issues has earned her many enemies. In 2004, she was attacked for some anti-Bush comments she made at an awards benefit for Moveon.org in New York in January. The following month, a club in Houston, Texas, received threats that Cho's performance would be picketed if she was left on the marquee. She and her friend and opening act, Bruce Daniels, showed up early at the Houston club to protest the protest, but the picketers never showed.

Again in 2004, in May, while performing at a corporate event, she was 10 minutes into her act when her mike was shut off and the band was instructed to start playing. The order allegedly came from the manager of the Omni Hotel, who was offended by her anti-Bush comments. This is what could happen when she did not have control of the mike, but thankfully it did not happen often. It was a brilliant decision after the debacle of *All-American Girl* to build a career on her own terms, to start her own production company and not have to depend on corporations that feel the need to censor artists. This decision to seek a career outside the mainstream did not seem to hurt Cho's ability to attract a huge, loyal following. "I don't have many expectations in terms of my career success in terms of doing anything that people would consider a mainstream success, like getting a TV show," she said. "All I care about is being good and doing what I enjoy and feeling like I haven't left anything behind." What a difference from 1994, when Margaret Cho was willing to do anything—including make herself deathly ill—just to please the ABC network executives.

Her business partner Karen Taussig notes what a difference artistic independence makes. "I'm not so arrogant to think there aren't comedians out there who can't make jokes about what's going on, but they can get to a certain point and then they stop," she said. "Jon Stewart's owned by Viacom. Bill Maher's owned by Time Warner. Everyone's owned by something and there's only so far they can go, and maybe if Margaret was also owned by a corporation, we'd be cutting stuff out, but she's not."

The DVDs of the collected episodes of *All-American Girl* was released in January 2006. Cho wanted to prepare to add her commentary track to the DVDs, so she watched all the episodes. She had not done so in a while, and she found it fun. A lot about the show escaped her memory—she surmised that maybe she had subconsciously blocked it out. She said in her blog:

> It actually wasn't bad at all. The problem with the show was that in the hysteria of this being the first Asian American family on screen, the writing was stuck in an identity crisis. If we are Asians, then are we funny? Are we racy funny or homey funny? Can we do this? Can we do that? Also, there seems to be a cast of thousands. I think it was because the idea of Asians on television was so outlandish that the executives thought to soften the blow by adding kids, parents, older siblings, twentysomething friends, cute white boys, and NO GAYS!!! Can you imagine???!!!
>
> Still, watching *All-American Girl* is pretty amazing, thinking of all the pressure we were under, and having no real vision of what it should be. It is like a pupu platter of jokes. One of everything, to please the uninitiated palate, an abrupt tutorial in Asian-American life as seen by a bunch of innocent bystanders. . . . All in all, I am coming to see that the experience was worth it, because I did get a startling education in race in Hollywood,

and why things don't work. I hope all the people who worked on the show get to see the DVD, and can look back and enjoy all the work we put into it.

Cho had grown enough since *All-American Girl* that she could now step back and critique the show without feeling emotionally invested. Unlike during Cho's *All-American Girl* days, her self-esteem was intact, her skin was thick, and her spirit resilient. She hardly flinched at the sacks of hate mail that poured into her e-mail inbox. The hateful words actually had the opposite effect—they egged her on. Occasionally she posts some of the hate mail on her blog and includes the senders' names and e-mail addresses. She is not surprised by their reactions. She interprets some of their anger as being a reaction to her refusal to subscribe to the notion that as an Asian woman, she should be silent and submissive. "Asian culture is very repressed," she told an interviewer from *The Age*, "and it relies upon its silence to maintain its wholeness. To break that silence is massively disruptive; it offends many people." Being called names does not hurt her—it only makes her feel stronger, because if name-calling is the opposition's best weapon, she believes, she will surely win the fight. She said:

> The hate mail I get is amazing, because it really shows how close to the surface racism is, sexism is, homophobia is, how much hatred there is toward the "other" in our society, toward the people who are different and the people who entitle themselves to comment on what is considered the majority. I think most of the anger is about, "Who do you think you are?" That's the thing, people cannot believe I entitle myself to this position of commenting on their society, how dare I do that—and that makes me feel I have succeeded, because my whole point is I have entitled myself to this position of commenting on all these things that I really shouldn't be. In the whole scheme of society, I should have no voice, but I do and not only do I have a voice, I have an indignant voice.

Margaret Cho has spent the latter part of her career tackling social and political issues. In 2006, she performed at the "Bring 'Em Home Now!" benefit concert, which was organized to give voice to the Americans who support the withdrawal of U.S. troops from Iraq.

Ironically, she learned from her own family how to be rebellious and how to speak out. She learned how powerful performance could be when she watched her Methodist minister grandfather reach a group of people by testifying and preaching. She learned from her parents, who resisted arranged marriages, about breaking the rules. She learned from her great-great-grandmother with the dinky pinkies how to be eccentric and compassionate and fierce all at once. She learned from her mother, who retained her Shinto beliefs, how to be compassionate.

Her parents finally embraced her decision to become an entertainer when they saw that she was clearly succeeding. "They had never, in their wildest dreams, expected that I would become what I've become, and they really relish the celebrity of it." Not that it mattered much anymore—Cho had finally learned to look inside herself for approval. She wrote:

> I spent most of my life really looking for the approval of others, and looking for being in the good opinion of others, and that was all I wanted. And that, you know, would always lead me to a dark and terrible place. And when I started listening to myself and believing in my own opinions and believing in my own thoughts and values, developing my own point of view, that was the best thing I could do.

Since her "comeback" after the failure of *All-American Girl*, it has been exciting to see Margaret Cho bloom into a personification of that year-round peony flower for which she is named— the hardy flower that thrives even in the coldest of winters. "I think my work now is an attempt to try and save America from itself," she said in 2004. What will she come up with next? To what end will she channel her sincerity, passion, compassion, intelligence and wicked humor? Longtime business partner Karen Taussig has a prediction: "I really believe she'll go down in history as being one of the greatest philosophers of our time."

FILMOGRAPHY

ACTOR
Bam Bam and Celeste (2005): Celeste
Nobody Knows Anything! (2003): Rental Car Agent
$pent (2000): Travel Agent (Shirley)
Can't Stop Dancing (1999): JoJo
The Tavern (1999): Carol
The Rugrats Movie (1998) (voice): Lt. Klavin
The Thin Pink Line (1998): Asia Blue/Terry
Face/Off (1997): Wanda
Pink as the Day She Was Born (1997): Donna
Fakin' Da Funk (1997): May-Ling
It's My Party (1996): Charlene Lee
Sweethearts (1996): Noreen
The Doom Generation (1995): Clerk's Wife
Angie (1994): Admissions Nurse #2

WRITER
Bam Bam and Celeste (2005)
Margaret Cho: Assassin (2005)
CHO Revolution (2004) (V)
Notorious C.H.O. (2002)
Grocery Store (2002) (V)
I'm the One That I Want (2000)

PRODUCER
Bam Bam and Celeste (2005) (producer)
Margaret Cho: Assassin (2005) (executive producer)
CHO Revolution (2004) (V) (executive producer)
Notorious C.H.O. (2002) (executive producer)
Grocery Store (2002) (V) (executive producer)
I'm the One That I Want (2000) (executive producer)

ACTOR ON TV

Sex and the City
> "The Real Me" (2001): Lynn Cameron (Cho plays a potty-mouthed fashion show coordinator who pressures Carrie into appearing in the show.) "I love that show and I really loved to be a part of it," Margaret said. "It was such a dream of mine." She mentioned to another interviewer: "I curse a mean streak. . . . It was very natural to me.")

The Nanny
> "Mom's the Word" (1998): Caryn

Duckman: Private Dick/Family Man
> "In the Nam of the Father" (1995) (voice): Mai Lin

Attack of the 5 Ft. 2 Women (1994): Connie Tong
> (aka *National Lampoon's Attack of the 5 Ft. 2 Women*)

AS HERSELF ON TV

The View (October 27, 2005)
16th Annual GLAAD Media Awards (2005)
Freedom to Marry (2005)
*Richard Pryor: I Ain't Dead Yet, *%$@!!* (2003)
The Sharon Osbourne Show (September 23, 2003)
Real Time With Bill Maher: Episode 1.15 (2003)
The Isaac Mizrahi Show (January 6, 2003)
The Anna Nicole Show: Holiday Special (2002)
The American Experience: Miss America (2002)
Life 360 (2001)
The Rosie O'Donnell Show (June 6, 2001, and June 16, 1999)
The Remarkable Journey (2000)
Celebrity Profile: Margaret Cho (1999)
Get Bruce (1999)
Comedy Central Presents: The N.Y. Friars Club Roast of Drew Carey (1998)
Pulp Comics: Margaret Cho (1998)
State of the Union: Undressed (1996)
Comic Relief VII (1995)
Out There in Hollywood (1995)
The Wonderful World of Disney: 40 Years of Television Magic (1994)

Late Show with David Letterman (September 27, 1994)
Asian America (1994)
Stand-Up Spotlight (1988)

CHRONOLOGY

1968 *December 5*   Margaret Cho is born in San Francisco. Soon afterward, Margaret's father is deported. Because her mother is unable to raise her on her own, Margaret is sent to Seoul, Korea, to live with her grandparents.

1971   Margaret, her father, and mother move together to San Francisco.

1983   Margaret is expelled from Lowell High School at age 15. She attends a summer stock program at a nearby university and makes some friends who are students at SOTA (School of the Arts). Instead of attending the local public high school, she auditions and is accepted at SOTA.

1984   Cho performs stand-up comedy for the first time at the Rose & Thistle, the San Francisco club above her parents' bookstore, Paperback Traffic.

1992   Cho moves out of her parents' house and to Los Angeles, into a house with a few other young performers. She begins to perform stand-up regularly at small clubs and on the road. She also auditions for TV and movie parts.

1993   The National Association of Campus Activities names Cho Best Campus Comedian. In two years, she performs on more than 300 campuses.

1994   Cho wins the American Comedy Award for Best Female Stand-Up, and *Rolling Stone* magazine names her "Hot Stand-Up."

1994–1995   Cho becomes the first female Asian American to have her own television series based on her life and stand-up. ABC picks up 13 episodes of *All-American Girl*, a prime-time sitcom about a rebellious Korean-American teen growing up in a typically conservative Korean-American household.

1994–1995 *All-American Girl* is panned by the critics, and Cho develops a severe eating disorder while under pressure from the network to lose weight.

1995 *All-American Girl* is canceled, and Cho hits rock bottom, drowning her misery in drugs and bad relationships.

TIMELINE

1983
Lowell High expels Cho. She enrolls in a high school for the performing arts.

1992
Cho moves out of her parents' house and to L.A. to pursue an entertainment career.

December 5, 1968
Cho is born.

1968

1994

1984
Cho performs stand-up for the first time at the Rose & Thistle, in San Francisco.

1994
Cho stars in the first sitcom about an Asian-American family, *All-American Girl*. The program is canceled after one season, and Cho is distraught.

1999 Cho rebounds and chronicles her experience with *All-American Girl* in a one-woman show, *I'm the One That I Want*, coproduced with manager Karen Taussig. The show premieres off Broadway and is made into a best-selling book and concert film. The film breaks the record for the most money grossed per print in movie history.

2000 *April* Gay and Lesbian Alliance Against Defamation (GLAAD) gives Cho its first Golden Gate Award, which honors a member of the entertainment or media community who,

1999
Cho rebounds with *I'm the One That I Want*, her first venture as an independent artist. For the show, the book, and the movie, she wins much critical acclaim.

2003
Cho marries performance artist Al Ridenour and launches a blog.

2004
Cho begins to campaign heavily in favor of same-sex marriage in response to legislative actions from those who are opposed.

1999

2006

2001–2004
Cho tours with three more shows—*Notorious C.H.O.*, *Revolution*, and *Assassin*. Each results in a concert film.

as a pioneer, has made a significant difference in promoting equal rights for all, regardless of sexual orientation or gender identity.

2001   Cho takes her new show, *Notorious C.H.O.*, on a 37-city national tour.

2002   Cho releases the *Notorious C.H.O.* movie, filmed on the last night of the 2001 tour.

2003   Her third sold-out national tour, *Revolution*, goes on the road. The show's CD is nominated for best comedy album of 2003. (It loses to a CD by George Carlin.) Cho marries performance artist Al Ridenour and launches a blog at http://www.margaretcho.com/blog.

2004   *February*   On Valentine's Day weekend, San Francisco Mayor Gavin Newsom initiates same-sex marriages and Cho appears at a same-sex marriage rally at the state capitol in Sacramento. She starts Love is Love is Love, (www.loveisloveislove.com), a Web site promoting the legalization of same-sex marriage.

2004   *July*   During the Democratic National Convention in Boston, Cho is uninvited to speak at a Human Rights Campaign fundraiser because of fear that her comments might cause controversy.

2004   *Fall*   The *Revolution* concert film premieres on the Sundance Channel, and in September, Cho takes her *State of Emergency* tour through the swing states of the presidential election. The ACLU honors Cho with its First Amendment Award in September. *State of Emergency* evolves into *Assassin*, which tours the United States, England, and Australia.

2004   Cho takes up belly dancing, eventually launching her own custom line of belly-dancing accessories, called Hip Wear, which are sold through her Web site.

2005 Cho completes her first narrative feature film, *Bam Bam and Celeste*, which she wrote and in which she costars, with friend and co-touring act, Bruce Daniels. It premieres at the Toronto Film Festival.

2005 *September* Cho releases her second book, *I Have Chosen to Stay and Fight*, a compilation of essays and prose about global politics, human rights, and other issues. In conjunction with the book's publication, she releases the DVD of *Assassin*, filmed at the Warner Theatre in Washington, D.C. It premieres on the gay and lesbian premium cable network Here! TV.

2006 *April* Cho begins hosting *The Sensuous Woman*, a traveling revue of burlesque, comedy, and belly-dancing performers that appears monthly in Los Angeles, San Francisco, and New York.

GLOSSARY

green room—The room backstage where performers hang out before and after they go onstage.

hambok—Traditional Korean dress worn since ancient times—it consists of either pants and a robe or a skirt and a robe. The garments are characterized by their simple lines, bright colors, and absence of pockets. Different types are worn for different occasions: for everyday, ceremonial, and special dress. Ceremonial dresses are worn on formal occasions, including a child's first birthday, a wedding, or a funeral. Special dresses are made for purposes such as those executed by shamans and officials.

improv—A performance given on the spur of the moment, without planning or preparation.

kill—In comedy, to do spectacularly well during your set—to be so incredibly funny that the crowd is doubled over with laughter and begging for more.

patriarchal—Referring to a society in which males are the heads of families and have ultimate authority.

pilot—A television program produced as a prototype of a series under consideration for adoption by a network.

set—In entertainment, one segment of a performance.

BIBLIOGRAPHY

BOOKS

Cho, Margaret. *I'm the One That I Want*. New York: Ballantine Books, 2001.

———. *I Have Chosen To Stay and Fight*. New York: Riverhead Books, 2005.

DVDS

All-American Girl, The Complete Series Starring Margaret Cho. Touchstone Pictures and Television, 2006.

Cho, Margaret. *I'm the One That I Want*. Wellspring, 2000.

———. *Notorious C.H.O.* Wellspring, 2002.

———. *Revolution*. Wellspring, 2003.

———. *Assassin*. Wellspring, 2005.

ARTICLES

Associated Press Newswire. "Outspoken Comedian Uninvited From Convention-week Event." Boston, July 22, 2004.

Benedictus, Luke. "No Business Like Cho Business." *Sunday Age* (Australia) (July 17, 2005).

Blowen, Michael. " 'All-American Girl' Fails Comic Cho." *Boston Globe, City Edition,* (September 14, 1994).

Carman, John. "Margaret Cho Breaks Ground in New Sitcom Role." *San Francisco Chronicle* (May 10, 1994).

Catalyst, Clint. "Bloody Cool? Reverend Al Ridenour's Ambulance Antics Define 'Sick' in the Best Sense of the Word." *Los Angeles Alternative*, vol. 4, no.15 (October 28–November 10, 2005).

Chang, Young. "Looking Ahead to Marriage, Margaret Cho Counts Her Chicken." *Seattle Times* (May 16, 2003).

Cho, Margaret. "Now That I've Started Belly Dancing, I Show Off My Navel Like Madonna During Her 'Lucky Star' Period." *Jane* (June–July 2006): pp. 136–137.

Cho, Margaret. "Presidential Cockfight." *In These Times* (October 22, 2004).

Downes, Lawrence. "Goodbye to Pat Morita, Best Supporting Asian" *New York Times,* (November 29, 2005).

Esther, John. "Margaret Cho Is a One-Woman Tornado." *Gay and Lesbian Review Worldwide* (March 1, 2006).

Halpern, Ashley. "Comedienne Margaret Cho Projects Her Individuality to Syracuse U." *Daily Orange, University Wire* (October 2, 2002).

Heldenfels, R.D. "Margaret Cho: Not Just Another Standup-Turned-Sitcom-Star." *Salt Lake Tribune, Knight Ridder News Service* (July 23, 1994).

Hepola, Sarah. "Margaret Cho Has Something on Her Mind: Herself." *New York Times*, Arts and Leisure, sec. 2, Theater (September 28, 2003).

Herron, Frank. "Serving the Underserved: Comedian Margaret Cho Brings the 'Politics of Beauty' to CNY." *Post Standard/ Herald Journal* (April 17, 2006).

Hoffman, Tod. "You Have to Laugh or Else You'd Cry. That's How Margaret Cho Approaches Her Comedy—And Laugh We Do." *Globe and Mail* (Montreal, Canada) (November 19, 2001).

Jasmin, Ernest A. "Margaret Cho's New Movie Shot in Seattle." *News Tribune*, Tacoma, Washington (August 9, 2002).

Katzman, Avram. "Margaret Cho and the 4th Wave of Feminism." *The Tablet* (October 2001).

Lauren, Jamie. "It's Cho Time: Interview With Margaret Cho." *NoHo LA The Magazine* (June 20, 2002).

Leff, Lisa. "For Margaret Cho, an 'All-American' Arrival: A Fresh New Comic Finds Fodder in Generation and Culture Gaps." *Washington Post* (September 11, 1994).

Multiple writers. "The It List: It Loudmouth, Margaret Cho." *Entertainment Weekly* (June 27, 2003).

Nash, Rob. "Comedian Margaret Cho on Belly Dancing, Marriage and the Holy City Zoo." *Austin American-Statesman* (June 9, 2005).

Nesti, Robert. "Getting to Know Her: A Very Funny Margaret Cho, Now Headlining in P'town, Thinks of Her Gay and Lesbian Audience as Her Core Constituency." *Bay Windows Online* (August 2001).

O'Sullivan, Michael. "Margaret Cho Gets Serious." *Washington Post* (August 30, 2002).

———. "Hilarious C.H.O." *Washington Post* (August 30, 2002).

Pacio, Nerissa. "Margaret Cho Exhales." *KRT News Service, Star Ledger* (June 28, 2005).

Richardson, Lisa. "She's a Stand-Up Academic for a Day: Comedian Margaret Cho Brings Her One-Woman Act to a UCLA Class on Race Relations." *Los Angeles Times* (March 19, 2001).

Savage, Dan. "Margaret Cho Gets a Dose of Savage Love." *Mother Jones* (May 1, 2002).

Schindehette, Susan. "Her Brilliant Korea." *People Weekly* (October 11, 1994).

Scott-Norman, Fiona. "Margaret Cho—Heat-Seeking Missile." *The Age* (Australia) (July 20, 2005).

Shankar, Radhika. "Profile—Margaret Cho, United States—All-American Girl: Korean-American Comic Smashes Asian Clichés in New U.S. Sitcom." *Far Eastern Economic Review* (December 15, 1994).

Stanborough, Denise. "Bleedin' Art." *Bizarre Magazine 105* (December 2005): p. 78.

Thill, Scott. "Emergency Revolutionary." Available online. http://www.alternet.org/story/19682/ (August 27, 2004).

Vivinetto, Gina. "The Margaret Cho You Don't Know," *St. Petersburg Times* (May 8, 2003).

Weilenga, Dave. "Jokers Wild." *New Times Los Angeles*, vol. 2, no. 18 (May 1–7, 1997): cover.

Youn, Soo. "For Comic Margaret Cho, Racism Leads to Freedom." *Reuters News* (August 15, 2002).

Zinder, Jac. "Clowns for Chaos: Cacophony's Carnival of the Absurd." *LA Weekly* vol. 16, no. 35 (July 29-August 4, 1994): cover.

RADIO INTERVIEWS

Conan, Neal. "Margaret Cho discusses her family background and career as a comedian." *Talk of the Nation*, National Public Radio (November 12, 2002).

Nyad, Diana. "Comedienne Margaret Cho Discusses Traveling and Being on Tour in a Different City Each Day." *Savvy Traveler*, National Public Radio (July 20, 2002).

Siegel, Robert. "Profile: Margaret Cho and Her Use of Comedy to Address Issues of Race Facing Asian-Americans in American Society." *All Things Considered*, National Public Radio (December 9, 2002).

Simon, Scott. "Comedian Margaret Cho Discusses Her Life and Her One-Woman Show 'I'm the One That I Want.' " *Weekend Edition*, National Public Radio (August 12, 2000).

Smiley, Tavis. "Margaret Cho Talks About Her New Stand-Up Comedy Film Called 'Revolution.' " *The Tavis Smiley Show*, National Public Radio (June 24, 2005).

TV INTERVIEWS

O'Brien, Soledad, anchor. "Comedian Margaret Cho Discusses Her New Book, *I'm the One That I Want*." NBC News: Saturday Today (June 23, 2001).

Seigenthaler, John, anchor. "Comedian Margaret Cho Discusses Gay Marriage on a Day When Comedian Rosie O'Donnell Is Married in San Francisco." CNBC: *The News on CNBC* (February 26, 2004).

Zahn, Paula, Kyra Phillips, and Sharon Collins, anchors. "Profiles of Melissa Etheridge, Margaret Cho." CNN: *People in the News* (May 24, 2003).

WEB SITES

Bruce Daniels Official Site. Available online. URL: http://www.brucedaniels.com.

Home of the Cacophony Society in Los Angeles. Available online. URL: http://la.cacophony.org.

Love is love is love.com: Margaret Cho's Marriage Equality Resource Site. Available online. URL: http://www.loveisloveis-love.com.

Margaret Cho.com. Available online. URL: http://www.margaretcho.com.

The Art of Bleeding. Available online. URL: http://artofbleeding.com.

FURTHER READING

Bark magazine, ed., *Dog Is My Co-Pilot: Great Writers on the World's Oldest Friendship*. New York: Three Rivers Press, 2004, "The New Girl" by Margaret Cho, p.31

Cho, Margaret. *I'm the One That I Want*. New York: Ballantine Books, 2001.

Cho, Margaret. *I Have Chosen To Stay and Fight*. New York: Riverhead Books, 2005.

Cho, Margaret. *www.margaretcho.com/blog*

Downs, Hugh, *My America: What My Country Means To Me, by 150 Americans by All Walks of Life*. New York: Scribner, 2002, p. 46.

King, Yolanda and Tate, Elodai, eds. *Open My Eyes, Open My Soul: Celebrating Our Common Humanity*. McGraw-Hill, 2003, p. 69.

DVDS

All-American Girl, The Complete Series Starring Margaret Cho. Touchstone Pictures and Television, 2006.

Cho, Margaret. *I'm the One That I Want*. Wellspring.

Cho, Margaret. *Notorious C.H.O.* Wellspring.

Cho, Margaret. Revolution. Wellspring.

Cho, Margaret Assassin. Wellspring.

WEB SITES

www.margaretcho.com
www.loveisloveislove.com

PICTURE CREDITS

INDEX